The
10C's

Model of Identity & Transformational Change

"Reconnecting, Reclaiming, Redefining & Celebrating All Aspects of Your Identity"

ULRIC RAPHAEL JOHNSON, PhD

Published by Lee's Press and Publishing Company
www.LeesPress.net

ISBN-13: : 979-8-9886270-2-9

PAPERBACK

MY TWIN BROTHER ERIC AND I

MANUELITA NUBELTA LEZAMA JOHNSON
JANUARY 5TH, 1922 – JUNE 14, 2015

Table of Contents

Acknowledgements

I would like to thank my wife, Kimble Carol Julien Johnson, for her continued support, care, and encouragement in developing my 10C's. I have the privilege of experiencing your 10C's. I continue to learn as you go through your own transformation process. Your love and your courage to love despite your physical and medical condition have been and continue to motivate me as I continue to develop as a black man, husband, father, and grandfather. Your commitment to being the best black woman, mother, and grandmother serves as a role model to me. This book is a combination of us both living our C's.

My dad Adolf Joseph French. Although I wish you were involved more in my life. I do appreciate you being in my life. Washing you in your army uniform, as a master sergeant directing all those soldiers during Trinidad and Tobago Independence Day parade. the way they respected and obeyed your command. Your expectations of them to respect themselves and each other left a lasting image impression of a strong Black man commanding and leading an army. It encouraged me to be disciplined. I especially remembered a very special conversation we had about your love for Mom and the excitement you had when you heard that you were going to have twins, and you said to me "Son you and your brothers were conceived from love", as always, up to today been words that lift me up during times I am at my lowest.

My daughter Kimberly, my son Kern, my brothers, my sisters, and uncle Christopher. You all have been my village that has provided me with the courage to continue the struggle for justice and peace.

Patti DeRosa, thank you for your insight and the work we have done together in educating others about the C's and how they could use the model in their own personal, professional, and organizational development. Those many workshops together made the model come alive and forced us to challenge our ability to walk the C's in every aspect of our lives.

Joyce Shabazz, my sister in spirit and love. Thank you for being such a strong Black woman and sister who articulates what it means to live confidently with one's C's.

Steven Brion-Meisel, my White ally in the struggle for justice and peace. You were not only my friend, colleague, and supporter encourager. A true example of a White ally, who is aware of his 10C's, and uses it to advocate for the elimination of racism, violence, and materialism. Your love, honesty, and proficiency in doing this work continue to be an inspiration to me. Your insistence that I write this book and the encouragement to overcome my trauma associated with the fear of writing is what makes this book possible.

Special thanks to Linda Brion–Meisels, Kristen Hendricken, Venisha Gilmer Jones, and Sonya Patton for your edits and suggestions.

John Braman, Matt Mink, Cathy Hoffman, Debra Cox, the members of Teens, Children, Parents, Volunteers and Interns of Teens Against Gang Violence, Graduate Students of Harvard Risk and Prevention Program, Undergraduate and Graduate students of Springfield College, School of Humans Services, Boston Campus, Teachers, and students that participated in the Global Youth Leadership Program, Teachers, Youth Leaders, Mental Health Practitioners, and Community Activists for the continuing evolution of the 10C's Model. Your collective wisdom, vision, and creativity continue expanding the depth and application of the 10 C's.

Foreword

The concept of identity, both on an individual and collective level, has become a prominent focus in the United States and globally. It is with great excitement that I introduce you to Dr. Ulric Johnson's groundbreaking book, "The 10 C's," which presents a new paradigm for understanding identity and transformative growth. This innovative Model recognizes that we are not static beings but rather dynamic and evolving entities. We continuously adapt and evolve in response to our surroundings, relationships, experiences, and aspirations. The 10 C's Model provides valuable insights into how we can harness this potential for change to manifest positive outcomes in our personal and professional lives.

The 10C's Model comprises ten fundamental components that shape our identity and influence our journey of transformation. These components are Color, Culture, Class, Character, Context, Courage, Confidence, Commitment, Conflict, and Community. Each element plays a specific role in helping us define our true selves, determine our aspirations, and chart a path toward their realization. Moreover, the 10C's Model equips us with practical tools and strategies to develop and fortify each component while overcoming challenges and barriers that may arise along the way.

"The 10C's" is not merely a theoretical framework; it takes readers on a personal voyage. Dr. Johnson shares his anecdotes and insights from applying the 10C's Model in his life and career. For instance, he reveals how Clarity assisted him in identifying his core values and purpose, how Commitment aided him in setting realistic and meaningful goals, how Courage empowered him to confront fears and embrace risks, how Creativity enabled him to discover novel solutions and opportunities, how Compassion fostered empathy

for both himself and others, how Connection facilitated the establishment of supportive and trusting relationships, how Communication allowed him to effectively express thoughts and emotions, how Collaboration promoted teamwork in pursuit of a shared vision, how Contribution enabled him to make a positive impact on communities and society, and how Celebration helped him appreciate achievements and learn from failures. He also invites readers to embark on their own journey of self-discovery and change potential through exercises, reflections, and actionable steps. By delving into this book, you will uncover how the 10C's Model can assist you in transforming yourself and your world for the better.

Author of Unlocking Legacies and Releasing Burden: How to Let Go of Generational Traumas & the Wounds that Keep Us Chained to the Past.

Dr. Gayle Crump Swaby

Prologue

This book on the C's of Identity, Awareness, and Transformational Change is an adaptation of the original 10C paper, the 10C's of Diversity, Awareness, and Social Change, written by Patti DeRosa and me.

This book focuses attention on the first 8 C's of Awareness: Color, Culture, Class, and Context and Change: Confidence, Courage, Commitment and Community, the Model that I wrote about in 1980. The model described a process that emphasizes the importance of me first truly loving who I am, being aware of my identity and the change process that started in Trinidad and Tobago and continued as a young Black male immigrant from Trinidad and Tobago. Coming to the United States, I realized very early that if I did not redefine my identity from the one presented to me by this country vs. the one given to me by my mom, I would not survive in Boston, MA or any part of the country.

My mom always made me feel loved and special, even as I struggled with some disabilities she and I did not understand. Mom's love was even more important as I navigated living in a new country that treated me and others that looked like me as less than human.

This country takes your focus away from being aware of your identity, which would lead you to better understanding and appreciating yourself. I still sometimes get distracted by multiple things, issues, and the daily oppression as a Person of Color while attending school, on the job, and just living in my community.

I soon realized that it is exactly how the system of white supremacy remains intact: using distractions and continuously presenting the delusion of change. It was easy for me to look at others and not myself—my relationships with myself. The original C's model was developed within a context where I was forced to focus on my C's in relation to my personal, professional, and political identities. The 10C's Model that Patti DeRosa and I later developed was a deeper analysis and explanation of the intersectionality of those C's. We added the C's of Character to the C's of Awareness and Conflict to the C's of Change.

The many presentations and discussions about the model have caused me to go even deeper in self-analysis and focus more on my personal identity and the changes that I needed to make. From back then, when I first arrived in the United States, right up to today, I grew more disappointed every day with the direction that this country and the world are going when it comes to ending Racism-White Supremacy. There are many advancements in technology, medicine, computers, etc., but we as a species are growing further away from our humanity.

*Technology continues to redefine our identity or C's daily. We are displacing or choosing to give up on our responsibility to be honest and genuine with ourselves, to where being dishonest and fake is the norm, from a place of **I=We** to a place of **I=I, LOVE to HATE.** I continue to reflect on my internal feelings about my identities as a man, father, husband, brother, grandfather, and, most importantly, human being. I reflect on why and how I developed the model in 1980 and how I have used my multiple identities to help others redefine their C's from a place of equality, inclusion, equity, and love. These terms are today's new buzzwords as if they never existed in the past. I continue to find the model extremely helpful in understanding how the complexity of my own 5C's of identity in relation to other individuals' C's across color, culture, class, and country.*

Many people, students, and friends have asked me to write a book on the 10C's, but I could not due to my writing phobia. My disability and early childhood traumatic experience and challenges, while attending school in Trinidad. I did not know I was dyslexic. I attend a school system, founded on colonialism principles and ideology. Those experiences affected my interpretation of my C's and my ability to write in general, much more my ability to write a book. Steven Brion Miesls, a friend and ally in the work of promoting non-violence, peace, and justice, and an excellent writer, offered to help me author a book on the C's. We started the process of writing the 10 C's book, but he unfortunately got ill with Cancer and transitioned before we could complete the book together. This re-writing of the 10C's article in the form of a book was a suggestion he made. He felt that revisiting and writing about my early experience and how it influenced the development of the model, without fear of spelling, grammar, etc.., would help me overcome my phobia of writing. I am taking his recommendation and taking this opportunity to share with you how I have used my own 10C's transformation to develop what I call the 10C's and Focused Counseling, in my work as a Cross-Cultural, Liberation, Antiracism Mental Health Counselor, Educator, Coach and Advocate, with a focus on helping People of Color recover from the trauma of internalized racism.

Introduction

When I give presentations on the 10C's, I start off with a 5C's of Identity introduction describing my awareness and love for my color, culture, class, character, and my context, where I was born and raised. The last "C" is especially interesting because my context entirely shifted when I immigrated from Trinidad to the United States at the age of thirteen. Anyone who immigrates usually goes through an instant shift in their 5C's, based on this country's definition of your C's. I, like a lot of immigrants, was forced to assimilate and accommodate a new definition of my C's, to survive in a new cultural context. During the presentation, I shared how I had to initiate a conscious redefining of Color, Culture, and Character. Then, I had to figure out the mental, intellectual, and physical context of where I chose to live and exist.

Every time I present on the C's, like writing this book has causes me to again stop and reflect on my growing up on the island of Trinidad and Tobago. This book summarizes this continuing journey of becoming aware of my 10C's. Growing up in Trinidad, I did not pay attention to my C's, because I was living in a context that did not require or encourage you to do so, because your time and energy was focused on the unconscious internalizing the racism you were being expose to through the media, in school, church and even in your home. It is only when I traveled outside the familiar context, like coming to the United States, that I began my journey of becoming aware of my 5C's.

The first "C" is Color. Color literarily refers to the color of my skin. But I also take it beyond skin color. Color can be thought of symbolically as physical or other attributes that I cannot change about myself. I am a heterosexual, Black African-Trinidadian male, 5'8" tall, who also happens to be an identical twin. These attributes will never change; they all describe part of who I am, part of what makes me Ulric. They all mean quite different things if I am in the inner-city neighborhood of Boston, MA lecturing at Harvard University, Assistant Dean Springfield College School of Human Services, visiting my home of Trinidad and Tobago, or spending time in another part of the world.

I was born in a small village called Point Cumana Big Yard in Trinidad in 1958. I am one of two identical boys; my mother had a total of eight boys and three girls. Being an identical twin gave me an eerie ability to watch someone whose color–whose core, unchangeable physical attributes – are identical to my own but whose life unfolded differently. It gave me the sense of my "self" being separated from my physical attributes. I would watch my identical twin get into trouble which I had managed to avoid, or flirt with girls while I went off on my own, sitting down by the sea to watch the sunset.

Early on in my life, I started asking questions like: Why are we so different, yet still have so much in common? Why did people only see my brother's likeness to me but not value our differences? Why were we always dressed alike, given the same toys, and (in some ways) even given the same dreams?

This lodged another especially important question in my head: "What are the parts that make up the self beyond the physical?" Answering these questions started a journey toward my self-awareness and transformation. Moving to Boston, MA, attached quite a different meaning to my physical attributes than had existed in my village in Trinidad, especially the "C" of Color.

The second "C" I talk about is Culture. Culture is the lens through which color is interpreted. Like all other cultures, my foundational culture of Trinidad, the culture of my youth, defined and assigned value and different weights to what made up my world and reality until I was thirteen. Coming to the United States forced me to make a cultural shift in how I was defined and how I felt I should be defined. I remember when my brothers and I were told we had one week to say goodbye to our friends, home, village, and reality. Our mother, who, together with my brothers, had waited in line starting as early as 4 a.m. and sometimes lasting the entire day to get a Visa to the United States, which was finally granted in January of 1973. So, we said goodbye to our friends, and, unbeknownst to u us at the time, we were saying goodbye to our way of living and experiencing the world.

We were heading to America to experience the real Bonanza, Leave It to Beaver, My Three Sons, and Happy Days. We were heading to where the streets were paved with gold. We were going to the land of opportunity and freedom, where you could be whatever you wanted to be. My world, my whole reality, was about to be redefined and changed. From the first day I landed in New York and headed to Boston, my introduction to the 'land of freedom' was cold and frigid. As I stepped off the plane, I could not believe that the air was so cold and that it was safe to breathe.

I later learned that coldness is the price you must pay to succeed. You were expected to breathe in the chilly air of systemic racism, internalized oppression, self-hate, and the negative racial identity to which you are told you belong and, at the same time, breathe out the air of love and admiration for the dominant group. I began to compare these two realities: the one I was familiar with and the one I was thrust into. I realized there were many similarities between the U.S. and Trinidad. Here, as in Trinidad, I still had that desire to be successful, loved, and have a sense of worth and control over my life. The difference was how I experienced those things growing up in Trinidad and how I experienced them in the

United States. Trinidad was a Context (the 5th "C") in which I got love and a sense of worth without having to give up my humanity. I attributed this primarily to my mom, grandmother, aunts, and uncle. They instilled in my brothers and me a sense of our self-worth, even while living under a colonialist British System. This system promoted the same self-hatred as Africans. Africans had been enslaved in Trinidad, and the culture there taught us to love and admire our White colonizers.

The church was one of the main instructors that promoted white supremacy and self-hatred through the indoctrination of the belief in the love of White God and hatred of a Black Devil. School was another institution where we saw the unconscious indoctrination of people in self-hatred. Where disciplinary practice of whipping students, like the whipping of enslaved Africans, as a form of discipline was reinforced and adopted by the general culture, I went to a school system where my success was predicated on being someone other than myself. In schools, we were taught to speak the King's English taught the British Governmental System, which was now our system, that not only sanctioned but encouraged the use of corporate punishment.

My mother and other parents, who were victims of the same colonized culture, and forced to internalize racism, often used the same verbal and nonverbal discipline approaches on their children. I remember being whipped often with belts and rods and verbally abused by teachers for small infractions. In retrospect, many of the beliefs, ideologies, and ways colonial slave masters used on my ancestors to keep power over the slaves were taught, practiced, encouraged, and rewarded in the Trinidad of my childhood. To go against these ideas took courage, commitment, and community. The cognitive dissonance they experience daily is a constant bat-

tle where they have to rely on their use of LOVE for their own individual humanity and relationship with others, despite initializing colonialism and racism to survive as a people. My village was my refuge while living in a world that denied my humanity, especially my African Trinbagonian identity, culture, and ideology.

Once I moved to the United States, I lost that refuge, that context of safety and validation, of the unified struggle in which we collectively took part. Trinidad was my home, with its warm weather and community costumes that focus on an ideology of I=We, grounded in the belief that we are all created equal by a God who gives every person the right to become all we can be as humans.

I was raised a Catholic and completed my first communion and confirmation. I remember my grandmother, mom, aunts – the whole family--being dedicated Catholics, even though the church encouraged men's dominance over women, White over Black, and materialism over authentic human relationships.

Christmas was my favorite holiday, despite the cognitive dissonance and contradiction. I looked forward to the season when everyone in the village for months would be busy preparing for Christmas: getting their houses ready by painting their houses inside and outside, new curtains, harm cooking with a wide variety of foods, and people singing and dancing. One of the most exciting things about Christmas was the gifts my brothers and I received from Santa Claus.

I remember asking myself who Santa Claus was, this White man with a white beard who, on December 25th, got credit for buying gifts for me. I knew it was my mom who had slaved for months to earn the money to buy the presents! Why did the God I was made to worship make it so difficult for those with African heritage?

How could God the almighty stand by as those with darker skin tones were denied material and non-material rewards while those who were lighter had easy access to them? What was the difference? Were we not the same?

When I came to the United States, I thought: Now I am in this big country where my brothers, my mom, and I will not have to deal with these things, and I will not have to ask these questions anymore. I quickly came to realize that what I had hoped would be different, was the same.

I experienced another form of the same violence that I experienced in Trinidad, an insidious, covert form of racism. My mom also had to continue combating sexism and protecting her children from not only the sticks and stones that break bones but also the words and the silences that leave internal scars and, if not addressed, kill your spirit.

I remember that the first time I was called a nigger was in the United States. The first time I was called poor and considered myself poor, occurred when I moved to the United States. It was the first time that I was made to feel different, I was even called an "Alien." I had an Identification card given to me by the government that stated that I was an "Immigrant Alien."

I realized true success is based on material possessions, how much money you make, the size of your house, or the car you drive. I realized I did not fully appreciate what I had while I was in Trinidad-- the love and the relationships I had with people who valued me for who I was without those material things. I quickly began to value the love and sense of worth that my mom worked so hard for my brothers and me to have.

But, as I grew older and reflected on what was and what was not important, I realized that even in this society, it is not what you have that is important, but the value that is culturally assigned to what you have. I am grateful to my mom for bringing me to this country because if she had not, I would not have realized how important her love and her struggle to raise me was to who I am today.

There are so many things I had in the United States that was completely different for my childhood experience in Trinidad. Back home I was not successful in school. I was called dumb and stupid, and I received a lot of corporate punishment due to -- what I did not know at that time -- poor eyesight and dyslexia, which affected both me and my twin brother. The diagnosis of my visual and learning deficits and getting glasses led me to redefine myself from being dumb and stupid to believing that I could learn and that what I had to say was valuable. It also made me realize the benefits of a good education.

Being able to see opened my eyes to a new world, one where I came to understand the cultural symbols of success in my new country: money, clothes, cars, advanced degrees, etc., were not easily accessible to people like me but were and appeared reserved for whites. Just like when I was growing up in Trinidad, I believed that these opportunities should be accessible to everyone regardless of color, culture, class, or context. True justice was the removal of all human-made barriers created, which prevented this from happening for everyone.

*The 5C's process of transformation required me to do several things: (a)develop **Confidence** in my C's, (b) **Courage** to stand up for my C's, (c) **Commitment** to the process of transformation, (d) my ability to engage in reflective struggle **Conflict** of choosing to be authentic rather than being superficial with myself and other, and (e) to build a **Community** that values and promotes LOVE for self and others, i.e., I=WE. Of these I would like to focus on the "C" of Conflict because it is essential to get to authentic communica-*

*tion. Conflict is what I would like to call the "cocoon stage" of transformation because it can be a dark, painful, and sometimes lonely time, but not without miraculous results. Conflict is a reflective struggle and a creative tension that promotes growth and justice in oneself and others. The key word here is "struggle." There must be an internal and external struggle in all four areas of oppression that we all experience, referred to as the 4I's of oppression, for true liberation and transformation to occur. They are Internal, Interpersonal, Institutional, and Ideological oppression. The internal struggle is where I experienced many inner conflicts between the image I saw in the mirror and the image American culture portrays as **beautiful, right, and good**. This leads to the internalization of the belief that you and others who look like you are not the norm.*

This dangerous undertaking sparks great tension and conflict in one's personal and professional lives. It's through utilizing the 5C's of transformation, with oneself and then with others, that we can bring about transformational peace and justice in this country and the world. Challenging the system of white supremacy like Dr. Martin Luther King, Jr., and many unknown advocates for justice. This struggle has taken many lives and has been the cost of challenging the ideology of a systems that promote racism in the world.

*It would be ideal to just go straight to the leaders of racist institutions in this nation and confront them about racism; demand them to stop denying our C's. But I soon learned that a more effective use of my time and energy was to start with myself, my **Circle of control**, and ourselves and extend out to the next **Circle of influence**, friends, and then the larger **Circle of Concerns,** country, and the world. We need to know that the Circle of Control, which is yourself directly and, at the same time, indirectly connected to the*

Circle of Concern, I=We.

The experience of living on a colonialized island that defined me and others that look like me as "less than" and "a loser" ended up serving me overall. I began redefining myself, my reality, and my relationships to self and others from a perspective of win-win, rather than win-lose. To do this, I had to realize there were multiple ways to look at what is "success."

I came to the realization that true success as an individual, as a people, comes from awareness and acceptance of one's C's -- the good and the bad. I needed to move toward valuing my humanity, and my perfection in being imperfect.

Then, and only then, did I realize the connection between myself and my C's with others and their C's.

This journey continues today. I still struggle and battle every day to live a life that is grounded in appreciation of my unique characteristics, my C's, and those of others, as I struggle to deny the pressures in this culture that support the opposite: dehumanization, objectification, idealization of a few limited ways of being instead of appreciation for the diversity of all humanity.

This all goes back to my mom and how she struggled to live her life. It speaks to the power of having someone in your life who can serve as a true role model of being human with all your imperfections, beauty, and resources necessary to survive anywhere you go.

I remember seeing my mom very closely, as she showed this internal sense of self and inborn survival skills. She was a role model of defiance and advocacy for freedom. She was actively involved in organizing the people in the village to vote when Trinidad and Tobago was fighting for its "independence," reclaiming our identity from the British colonial government.

She had a unique gift of connecting with young people. She played sports with them, she disciplined them, loved them, shared with them, and was their "Village Mom." I also saw this from most of the people of the village. They looked out for us and each other.

Every day I try to be a role model like my mom. Despite all the internalized racism and sexism inside me, I continue to work hard to become more aware of this oppression and to continue understanding that it does not have to be that way. I try to be a role model not of perfection but an individual in continually transforming and reclaiming my humanity, my experiences, and my C's with all their beauty and imperfections.

*This is what I have defined as my life work and what I try to role model to the people I interact with, both personally and professionally. It is the process I call **transformation**, and it informs my professional, personal, and political role as a teacher, counselor, and advocate.*

It is about helping people become free from what I call mental slavery and oppression, and it involves awareness and appreciation of one's 10C's. We live in a culture that preaches materialism, racism, and violence. However, with the proper support, attitude, knowledge, and awareness you can begin to see that you - and only you - can decide if you want to be free or enslaved. You begin to realize that there is a whole other way of existing, existing without having to resort to being dependent on violence, racism, or material things as a way of making yourself superior to others. The need to be superior to others is part of enslavement.

In Trinidad, we are encouraged to worship the people who taught us a system of oppression, the one that we all internalized. As Willie Lynch, a slave owner who experimented on the ways of mentally controlling the slaves in his Jamaica plantation three hundred years ago, once said. "Envy and jealousy are more powerful than love and admiration in controlling your slaves and their commitment to being enslaved. You must train them to envy and hate each other, love, and admire only you, their slave master."

We have a lot of people, places, and things to which we all are enslaved. I realized this when I came to the United States and had to overcome envy and jealousy of my own. Even my mom had to overcome these evils. As people of color, we choose to be envious and jealous of each other more than love and admire each other. This internalized self-hatred prevents us from having a genuine love relationship with ourselves and those who look like us. We will voluntarily give up freedom rather than share it between ourselves and others.

This is the cycle of internalized oppression, racism, and the Post Traumatic Slave Syndrome (PTSS). The 10C's is one way I believe I can contribute to the struggle to stop the cycle of hating ourselves and each other. I/We need to combat the influence of Willie Lynch!

We need a way of counteracting internalized oppression, racism, and PTSS. The C's allows us to experience the opposite, to understand and reclaim our humanity. Self-hate is additive, and denial is the number one sign of an addiction. The only way that you move toward recovery is to first admit your addiction to this way of thinking and existing. Then, make a conscious decision to stay away from people, places, and behavior that support these negative ways of thinking and existing.

The 10C's Focused Counseling is a process that uses the concept of recovery, grounded in LOVE for self and others in addressing internalized oppression. It is a process where people of color, can explore their C's and experience valuing them, but not at the expense of others. It is a struggle to reclaim your humanity in a world that is so conscious and deliberate in dehumanizing you and to see how you take part in that process. We, People of Color, continue to work more than one job, to pay for things we do not need; we continue to look for validation and acceptance from the same system that dehumanizes us, and the list goes on.

*You are not in recovery until you address the beliefs that continue to inform your thinking and behavior. This is like the concept of a dry drunk when one is recovering from alcoholism. Racism and internalized oppression, like all diseases of addiction, are slick. It is like an eel. You grab it and think, "I got it! -- Then you look in your hands, and they are empty. We are not static; we go back and forth. The process of forgiveness, empathy, and making amends -is a continual process. This process is LOVE in action and serves as the foundation of the 10C's Focused Counseling process. LOVE stands for being able to **L**isten- be **O**pen, **V**ulnerable, and **E**mpathetic, first to oneself and then to others.*

Genuine LOVE is one of the gifts that children give us all. I keep a quote in my office: "The momentous events of the world are not wars, elections, earthquakes, and thunderbolts. The momentous events of the world are babies because each child comes with the message that God is not yet discouraged with humanity and is still expecting goodwill to incarnate in each human life."

Children start out without any barriers to their humanity. That is why my mom loved being around children, and now I do as well. They help keep faith in humanity by reminding us that the Creator has not given up on us. If we give up hope in humanity, we have given up ourselves and each other.

Part One of the Journey: Growing up in Trinidad and Tobago

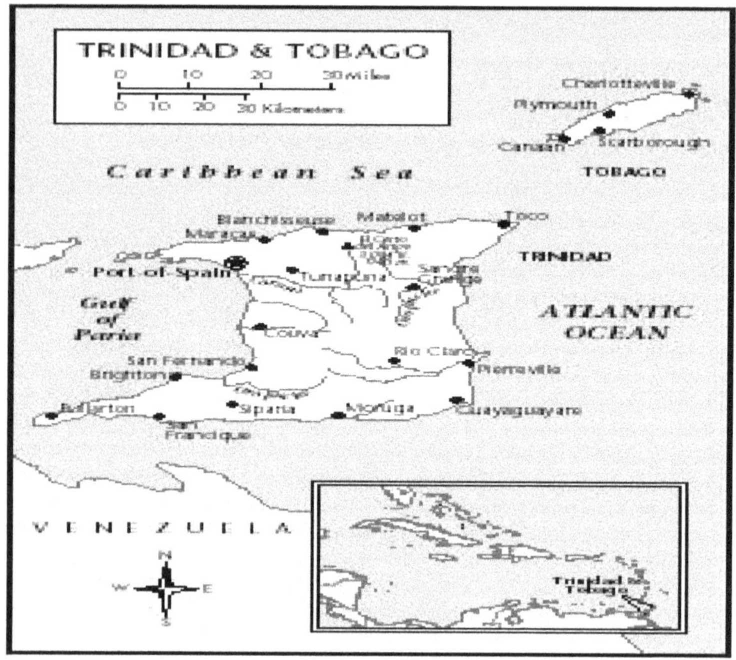

A. Brief Explanation of the Islands

Depending upon which island in this twin–island state is being discussed, the cultural name is "Trinidadian" or "Tobagonian." Alternatively, some people refer to citizens of the Republic of Trinidad and Tobago as "Trinidadians" or "Trinis," or occasionally, to be inclusive, as "Trinbagonians.

"Trinidad was named by Christopher Columbus on his third voyage to the New World. On the morning of July 31, 1498, he saw what appeared to him as a trinity of hills along the southeastern coast. The island was called Iere, meaning "the land of the hummingbird," by its native Amerindian inhabitants. Tobago's name is

derived from Tabaco (tobacco in Spanish).

Trinidad (but not Tobago) is ethnically heterogeneous. Trinidadians and Tobagonians of African descent are called "Negro," "Black," or "African." Trinidadians of Indian descent are called "East Indian" (to differentiate them from Amerindians) or "Indian." More recently the terms "Afro-Trinidadian" (or "Afro-Tobagonian") and "Indo-Trinidadian" have gained currency, reflecting heightened ethnic claims to national status.

Trinidadians of European ancestry are called "White" or "French Creole There are several designations for those of Black–White ancestry, including "Mixed," "Colored," "Brown," and "Red" among other terms.

B. Growing up in Trinidad and Tobago

Bathing Baby   Bleaching Cloths   Roasting Breadfruit   House in Trinidad

Playing the steel pan   Playing Cricket   Playing mass at Carnival

My journey begins in Trinidad-Tobago where I was born on October 24, 1958, together with my twin brother, Eric. He was the opening act, born three minutes before I made my grand appearance. This sets the scene and context for the 10C's framework, and it reminds me all the time that our work of being human "starts with the self." Who was this young man who came to Boston at the age of thirteen in the winter of 1973?

I have ten brothers and sisters, shared by three fathers. But at the center of our world was one mom, who was the rock (and the spirit) of this large family. Manuelita Johnson, my mom, made her transition on June 14, 2015, and is now with the ancestors. She was then and is now the matriarch of the family.

While growing up in Trinidad-Tobago, I remember my mom as much more than a mom. Although she did not finish school, she was a respected leader of the village. My mom was called Ms. TI ("Tiny Eyes" -- a nickname given to her by grandparents' due to the tiny eyes she had as a baby) and was known as Ms. TI by everyone in the village of Point Cumana, Carnage, Trinidad. My mom was the center of my family and other children in the village as well! For all of us children, the phrase "It takes a village..." was true.

Life in the village was good in many ways, filled with soccer and mangoes, family, friends, and the blue ocean. But life in school was a unique experience for me. I struggled in school. I did not pass the "common entrance" required to enter college, the next level of education, or "school leaving exams" equivalent of graduating high school, all part of the British colonial heritage educational system in Trinidad and Tobago. This brought me humiliation and physical punishment, and I was told it will lead me to a future as a laborer. I remember being called "dumb" and "stupid" by teachers and classmates for over twelve years because I often got bad grades and could not read.

Growing up in Trinidad and Tobago, to me, was living in a colonial society. I lived a dual existence, a dual reality. One reality was that of the colonized systems the British sanctioned to keep their dominance, but right alongside that was the reality of the subculture – a culture that was practiced by most citizens. I refer to this as the "TRUE CULTURE" of Trinidad, one rooted in the African identity, tradition, and reality.

We, as children, look forward to the weekends! That was the time away from what I consider the British school's plantation and educational system of the indoctrination of white supremacy. Weekends were the birthday parties, christenings, weddings, and even funerals that were wonderful to attend. All these events were opportunities to celebrate community. To celebrate life, everyone was welcome. For example, when someone died, the neighborhood would gather to aid the family experiencing the loss. We even dug the grave and helped plan the funeral. We would all bring food, drinks, music, yes, even music, because days before and after the funeral people would visit the wake house and play music, sing hymns, eat, drink, play cards, etc.

Whatever suffering or sorrow being experienced due to the loss of someone was an affirmation of the value of human life, the gift of music, food, and love! Sometimes it was a pure celebration! We would do the same for birthdays, weddings, anniversaries, etc.

The celebration of Carnival was another opportunity to experience community. I remember participating in Carnival, one of the largest celebrations in the world. All those weeks costumes were being made, and the many steel pan bands were practicing. The steel pan was invented in Trinidad and Tobago, the only acoustic instrument invented in the 20th century. ("The History of the Steel Pan") It is an instrument invented to replace the banning of the Jimbe, an African drum used in celebration and often used as a form of communication. So, here you have through the desire to maintain the African celebration of life, the invention of a new, gorgeous, alive form of musical instrument the Steel Pan, rising from suffering, enslavement, and the denial of life. This is the con-

This was the foundation of my youth: events and activities that I/we collectively took part in with others that looked like me on the Islands where I/we were the majority— where, from the trash collector to the prime minister, many of my fellow citizens reflected my C's. My family, together with the love of a mom helped me connect to my humanity while I continued to live in a context that repeatedly worked to deny me and others that look like me that same humanity.

To maintain that humanity, one must have a mom who is willing to be in a relationship with the village, one must have a mom that values what she brings to the village and what the village has to offer. I admire my mom's consistent involvement with the community, for the love she had for her country and for traditional and nontraditional cultural practices. She had the ability to use the best of both cultures to the benefit of self in relationship to others.

While I was growing up, I remember my mom intervening in domestic disputes, at times putting her life in danger. In one incident I saw my mom put herself between a man whom we knew was beating his wife and who was about to hit her with a brick which would have killed her.

My mom held the man's hand and spoke to him saying, "I watched you grow up. I know your mom. I watched you and your wife both love each other and raise your children. Think about what you are doing." She continued like that until he was able to calm himself down. I also remember another time when she did the same thing but this time it was between two men who were fighting, and one had a machete. My mom was a victim of domestic violence, and at times almost killed.

All this I believe is what makes me value the complexities of being human. It is not easy to undo the legacy of the evil and violence that still exist in Trinidad and Tobago. It is a beautiful country; it has a beautiful culture shaped by its experience with the evils of slavery and oppression.

Part Two of Journey: Moving and Living in Boston

Picture of family sendoff of my brothers and mother leaving for the United States

Like many immigrants, my family first sent a scout: my sister Jean, who volunteered to leave her three children with her mom to work in the United States.

Her reports suggested that Boston was the direction my family should follow. So, one day in January, with a large family send-off, mom, my two brothers, Eric, and Joseph, and I boarded an airplane headed for Boston.

Imagine this scene: you are a thirteen-year-old Black boy arriving at John F. Kennedy Airport, (JFK) in New York in 1973. It is the middle of January, and the weather is cold, sub-zero, and you are crying because you cannot feel your ears, and it was colder than you ever thought was possible. This was your very first plane ride, but it was no ordinary trip or vacation. This plane took you from the warm, sunny, tropical island of Trinidad and Tobago to your new home in the United States -- Boston, Massachusetts.

I distinctly remember when we arrived at JFK airport, it was so cold that my brothers and I did not want to leave the airplane: I recall my younger brother, Joseph, crying, "I can't feel my ears!" Mom's reply was, "Don't touch them because they will fall off!"

Driving from the airport to Boston, we all could not believe we were riding underwater in the Callahan Tunnel that connected East Boston to the City of Boston. When we arrived at my sister's house, there were indoor flush toilets! I learned that all the houses had indoor toilets. We were raised with an outside toilet called a latrine back home.

The physical coldness we experienced was an icy indicator of the psychological coldness we came to feel as immigrants in this new and confusing place where everything was different. I had heard that in America, the streets were paved with gold and that opportunity was open to everyone who was willing to work for it. Everything here was so much bigger than at home. The buildings were taller, the streets were wider. Everyone had a big car, a T.V., and having indoor plumbing and toilets is expected rather than a luxury.

Things that did not seem particularly important at home in Trinidad - like being Black (most everyone around you was) and having an "accent" (which was not really an accent at all because everyone else spoke that way, too) grew to take on new significances in my life. In school, I got bombarded with negative stereotypes and comments about who I was and everything that I valued.

I was called "different," "stupid," "island boy," "foreigner," "alien," and for the first time in my life I was called what may be one of the most hurtful words in the English language, "nigger." I was caught between worlds - not accepted by Whites, yet not fitting in with Black Americans either.

Questions and contradictions filled my mind. What was wrong with being Black? What was wrong with being an immigrant from Trinidad and Tobago? What was wrong with the way I spoke, my accent? Why did these people feel that they had the right to hurt me and my brothers? Verbally and physically. Where was the America that everyone spoke about, that you heard about from fellow Trinbagonians that came home on vacation?

I should have known that the picture that was presented to me was not true, but this delusion was sold to us, and we believed it while we were still at home. Even the snow on the ground in the United States was not what it appeared to be. It was not what one saw on postcards or in the movies. In fact, it was cold, heavy, and even turned dirty after staying on the ground for just a couple of days. I continued to have these questions as my brothers, and I continued to be bullied by African American youths. Then came forced busing when we had stones and bottles thrown at us by White adults. At the same time, we were called "niggers" and "monkeys" while we rode school buses to and from schools.

One significant person in my life during this time was Mr. Thompson, the middle school teacher who oversaw my brother and me having our eyesight examined. The later diagnosis of severe vision problems leads to my twin brother and I having to get glasses -- "Coco Cola Glasses" because of how thick the lenses were! But these glasses opened a new world of academic success for us. It was amazing! I was not dumb and stupid as I had been led to believe for over twelve years back in Trinidad. But the success I achieved in school now led to more teasing and name-calling, including being accused of "acting White."

I came to realize that the truth was that Boston streets were paved with cold rather than gold! Our first apartment in Matta-pan was full of roaches! And we had a heating system that was so bad that we had to have the oven on all night, and we all had to sleep in our winter coats.

I saw my mom live in daily fear for my brothers and me as we went to an inner-city school found in the middle of Boston. How could she protect her children? How could she go to work and not be worrying about them, always looking at the news to see and hear what was happening next?

Then my mother heard of METCO, a program started by other parents of color who were concerned about the inadequate education as well as the safety of their children in the Boston Public Schools. The goal was to send inner-city students of color to suburban schools that would provide them with a good education and at the same time ensure them more safety. My mom, like other parents of color, felt that METCO was the answer to her concerns. Acceptance to the program was, and still is, extremely competitive. In fact, she had heard that parents register their children before they are born just so they can get a better chance of being accepted.

Luck had it that a friend of a friend of my mom knew of someone that worked in the METCO office, and my mom's application was accepted. My brothers and I were interviewed and accepted. Our acceptance was due to our good academic performance, our good behavior, recommendations from our teachers, and especially how we were taught (back home) to carry ourselves when communicating with adults.

Not only were my brothers and I accepted into METCO, but eventually we were part of the first cohort of METCO students to be sent to Rockland High School. Rockland High was an all-white school located forty-five minutes from Dorchester. This meant that my brothers and I had to get up at 4 a.m. (vs 7 a.m.) so we could be on time for the school bus. That meant that at 4 a.m., even before sunrise, i.e., in the dark, my brothers and I waited for a school bus, sometimes in the freezing cold.

Rockland felt like another country for my brothers and me. We again felt like unaccepted immigrants from another country, experiencing the same aggression we had experienced in the Boston Public Schools: the looks, the teasing because of our accents, and the name calling: "nigger," "island boy," "foreigner," "immigrant," etc.

Thank God I was not alone! I had two brothers that shared the same experience.

The painful experiences helped us grow closer to each other. We were now getting these attacks on our C's from both the African American METCO students and now also the White students.

Looking back, I strongly believe that my brothers and my experience of being raised in Trinidad and the uncompromising love of my mother gave us the courage to make it through the days of attending Rockland High School.

The values of respect for teachers and adults we showed, the value for education we showed, and the positive use we made of the opportunities that Rockland High School provided, which was quite different from the Boston Public Schools we had attended, made the Johnson brothers stand out. We were even recruited for the varsity soccer team but later realized that it was due to the stereotype that all Caribbean males could play soccer. We did play soccer in Trinidad, but not at the varsity level. Back home, we could not make our school soccer team. We played better than the other players because Rockland had a reputation for having a bad soccer team. So here we were varsity soccer players, and the more we got to play, the better we became.

In fact, the Johnson brothers stood out for still a different reason. We became soccer stars, scoring multiple goals, and our names were always mentioned on the school announcement system. This led to increased self-esteem and group esteem as Trinbago-nians. And all this led to good academic performances, scholar-ships, grants, and acceptances to college.

B. Still Living in Boston

My family wife - Kim, daughter - Kimberly, Son - Kern and granddaughter-Tajiah

I currently live in Dorchester, in the inner city of Boston. I have held faculty positions at Harvard University, Springfield College; an Assistant Dean position at Springfield College; and I am the Director of a Youth Leadership Program. In addition, I am the manager of a steel band, and I run a private mental health group practice. I have lived through two terms with a Black president of this country, where he and his Black family lived in the White House for eight years.

I am living in a country with a White elected President Donald Trump, who before and during his election explicitly expressed his dislike for the former Black President Barack Obama and his policies, such as universal health care, criminal justice reform, immigration policy reform, and civil rights.

The first thing President Trump did when he came into office in 2016 was to begin to undo the progressive changes that the former President had made. In fact, he implemented and promoted policies that reinforce racism, sexism, homophobia, and our im-migration laws. He promised and continues to support a White Su-premacy agenda. This has contributed to creating a context that has led to an increase in unarmed, Black males being killed by po-lice without any consequences.

Now let me be clear that this reality of increased homicides by police was still occurring, even while there was a Black President in the "White House". The economic, health and education disparities are also a continuation of policies under both administrations, just as they were when I first arrived in the United States in 1973.

I still might ask the same questions I asked in 1973: What is wrong with being Black? What is wrong with being an immigrant from Trinidad and Tobago? What is wrong with the way I speak, my ac-cent? Why do these people feel that they have the right to hurt me and my brothers? Verbally and physically? Where is the Amer-ica that everyone spoke about, that you heard from fellow Trinbago-nians that came home on vacation? But now, I can confidently an-swer my own questions. The answer has to do with the United States establishment, preservation, and promotion of Racism – White Su-premacy.

I have worked in various capacities since 1990 as a diversity edu-cator, activist, college professor, administrator, youth and family advocate, psychotherapist, mental health counselor, and consult-ant. As I continue my own journey in this country at the age of sixty-two, I continue to see the need to be aware of and study the power differences in this culture, especially around race, culture, gender, class, and sexual orientation.

I continue to work, in various roles, with a diversity of people from various parts of the world. The relationships and experiences with these people have caused me to deepen my understanding of how important the process is of coming to understand identities, our individual identities and our social group identities. I am still amazed by the power differences that exist in this country due to race, culture, gender, class, sexual orientation, and other aspects of diversity.

I have come to love this country and at the same time am ever more disappointed with her inability and willingness to make amends. The 10C's model has continued to provide me and others with a means by which to understand the complex social and political meaning of the intersectionality of self, group identity, and institutional-systemic power.

The term Diversity is still used loosely and often, often without precise definition or purpose. It is still used as a euphemism for an individual's race or gender identity to soften the impact of discussing institutional, systematic, and cultural racism and sexism directly.

Diversity is used to include every human identity difference under the sun: Apple vs. Android users, Christians vs. Muslims, Progressives vs. Conservatives, and every other variable. Diversity is a term that can mean everything and nothing.

The current attention being given to the issue of gender identity is an attempt to answer some fundamental questions about human identity and experience. Who are we? What are we? Whose descriptions define us? How do those definitions develop and affect us? Why are our identities important and why should we explore them at all? How do they affect the way we see ourselves and lead our lives? Who has access and power and to whom are they denied or restricted? Why is there such division among people? Why can we come together?

These questions have often remained unspoken, and with the start of the Black Live Matter Movement was taking center stage. It was no longer taboo to discuss these issues; they were for a period openly spoken about and no longer silenced because most of the country feels these are questions that need to be answered.

Then we chose Trump as President, and now at the national and local levels have become so much more White Supremacy focused, especially after he lost the election. Books about People of Color's past experiences of systemic, cultural, and institutional oppression are being banned and taken off the shelves in libraries and public-school curricula.

Oppression, be it racism, sexism, heterosexism, or any other form has continued to fragment our identities and our nation. The 10C's model is an attempt to reconnect, reclaim, redefine, and celebrate all aspects of who we are. It is only by embracing all parts of ourselves that we can become whole, empowered beings who can work to end the oppressions that hurt and divide us.

Part Three of the Journey: THE 10 C'S MODEL: *The Birth of Four C's: Boston College*

*The 4C's framework (**color, culture, class, and context**) was my focus during my time as an undergraduate at Boston College. These were the C's of my identity that I saw constantly being attacked and defined in such negative ways, though I was living in what I saw as my adopted home where I should have been accepted and valued. I became even more aware of these attacks when I was a college student and met both other immigrants as well as students of color who were born here.*

I joined the efforts of other students of color to create an AHANA (African American, Hispanic, Asian, and Native American) alliance as well as a Black Studies Center and library at Boston College. Together we worked to understand the role of institutional structures that affirmed or attacked identity. This experience caused me to take a deeper look at my "4 C's" in the light of my own identity and journey, as well as within the political contexts of colonialism and racism. After college, this framework became a valuable tool in my work as a staff psychologist with clients and colleagues at Boston City Hospital (now Boston Medical Center). The fifth "C" was not far away; it was born through collaborative work across cultures and gender with Patti DeRosa.

<u>Ulric and Patti: The Birth of the Ten C's.</u>

One day back in 1984, I was approached to be a member of a planning committee for a conference on youth violence in Boston. I also was asked to sit on a panel at that conference. Here, I was introduced to Patti DeRosa, who, in addition to working as an affirmative officer for City Hospital, conducted training on diversity and youth leadership.

*There was an immediate connection personally, professionally, and politically. Patti and I initially discussed the "4C's of Identity" (**color, culture, class, and context**). This led to many discussions about our own identities; mine as a Black male from Trinidad and Tobago and Patti's as a White female living in the United States. These discussions led to the development and expansion of the four C's: Color, Culture, Class, and Context, to the **10C's Model of Awareness and Change**: the 5Cs of Awareness: Color, Culture, Character, Class, Context, and the 5C's of Change; Confidence, Courage, Conflict, Community.*

We both eventually went on to form the Cross-Cultural Consultation group, with the 10C's serving as the main theory behind the workshops, trainings and consultation on diversity and multicultural education that we presented to schools, corporations, and community groups.

African Heritage: The Nguzo Saba

One very influential part of my journey in the development of the 10C's and in defining my own identity was the encounter with what some have called the Black National Liberation Movement of the 1960s and 1970s. This movement had many streams – separatist (Nation of Islam), educational (Black Freedom schools), political (SNCC), religious (African Liberation churches), militant and economic groups (Black Panthers), and cultural traditions (Dr. Maulana Karenga's introduction to Kwanzaa).

One cultural aspect of this movement was a re-turning and re-honoring of African heritage and tradition – including the creation of the winter ritual Kwanzaa, the resurgence of West African clothing and music, the re-telling of African myths and a renewed interest in African culture.

Not surprisingly, this movement was connected to several other intellectual, academic, and economic changes that were in turn connected to broader social changes (like the United States Civil Rights Movement, the growth of Feminism and LGBT activism, anti-war and anti-colonial movements, a general interest in alternatives to market capitalism, etc.). My study of identity was shaped within this broader context – including the development of an academic field focused on identity development.

The Nguzo Saba are the seven principles that inform Kwanzaa. Dr. Maulana Karenga called the Nguzo Saba "the Ten Commandments of Black Liberation" because he believed cultural changes were critical to an authentic Black Liberation movement. These principles reflect important aspects of African culture, but they also supplied important guidelines for those who look to create communities of love and justice anywhere and anytime.

<u>Summary of the Seven Principles:</u>

Umoja (Unity): *to strive for and keep unity in the family, community, nation, and race. ("Umoja: Unity To strive for and maintain unity in the family, community ...")*

Kujichagulia (Self-determination): *To define ourselves, name ourselves, create for ourselves and speak for ourselves. ("Kujichagulia (Self-Determination)*

Ujima (Collective Work and Responsibility): *To build and keep our community together and make our brothers' and sisters' problems our problems and solve them together. ("Ujima Village")*

Ujamaa (Cooperative Economics): *To build and keep our own stores, shops, and other businesses and to profit from them together. ("Ujamaa: Cooperative Economics in the Black Community").*

"Nia (Purpose): *To make our collective vocation the building and* *developing of our community in order to restore our people to their traditional greatness." ("Nia – To make our collective vocation the building and developing of ...").*

Kuuma (Creativity): *To always do as much as we can, in the way we can, to leave our community more beautiful and beneficial than we inherited it. ("Kuumba (Creativity) | AfricanAmerica.org").*

Imani (Faith): *To believe with all our heart in our people, our parents, our teachers, our leaders, and the righteousness and victory of our struggle.*

The Nguzo Saba supplied an important new resource for me in my personal, professional, and political journey – a kind of roadmap or a set of principles that provides guidelines for a young Black man looking to understand his personal and group identities and to use that understanding to promote positive social change.

In this way, the Nguzo Saba became both a frame and a bridge for my work. As a frame, it places individual identity development in broader cultural and political contexts. For example, the principle of Kujichagulia (self-determination) is a group as well as individual process – because it also connects to Ujamaa (cooperative economics) and Ujima (Collective Work and Responsibility).

The Nguzo Saba principles have collective as well as individual implications and applications. They connect the individual with the group – and with broader spiritual connections as well. In European terms, they reflect Martin Buber's "thou" connection (i.e., "I am fundamentally connected to you").

In African tradition, the Nguzo Saba connects with the principle of Ubuntu: I = we. African tradition (in the form of the Nguzo Saba, Ubuntu, and the Black Cultural Liberation practices) supplied a communal or collective vessel or frame for my efforts to develop an inclusive, culturally competent approach to identity development –

and to the application of this understanding to the work of social change.

*As a bridge, the Nguzo Saba makes several important contributions. First, it connects the individual with the community. Second, it supplies action steps for using a positive identity (whether it is rooted in African tradition) in the service of social change. Here, the Nguzo Saba bridges the Five Cs of Awareness (Color, Culture, Class, Character, and Context) to the 5C's of Change (**Commitment, Confidence, Conflict, Courage, and Community**).*

Third, the Nguzo Saba provides a cross-cultural bridge – it connects African tradition with contemporary social/political change principles that include but are not limited to the principles of African tradition. For example, efforts to create democratic schools or communities draw on the Nguzo Saba and work collaboratively with youth to change social service and welfare patterns so they are liberating rather than oppressive.

The Nguzo Saba guides us to find new family and spousal roles that open collaboration within the family and to step back from market capitalism in the way we use our economic resources (think about car shares and cooperative housing). In other words, the Nguzo Saba – like the 10C's – supplies at least a potential cross-cultural and cross-generational set of principles that can be used to foster community and social change.

Despite its origins in a potentially separatist cultural movement, the Nguzo Saba calls us to step outside the confines of exclusivity of "us against them." In this way, the Nguzo Saba points to an ideology (or belief system) that is inclusive, cooperative, liberating, and transformational – themes that we will explore later in this book.

The 4I's: The Process of Oppression:

Another very influential part of my journey in the development of the 10C's and defining my identity was understanding the process of my oppression and the sources of my internalized racism, internalized colonialism, and self-hatred. It supplied the cause and, at the same time, the solution for confronting the fundamental ideology that supports the process.

THE 4I's OF OPPRESSION

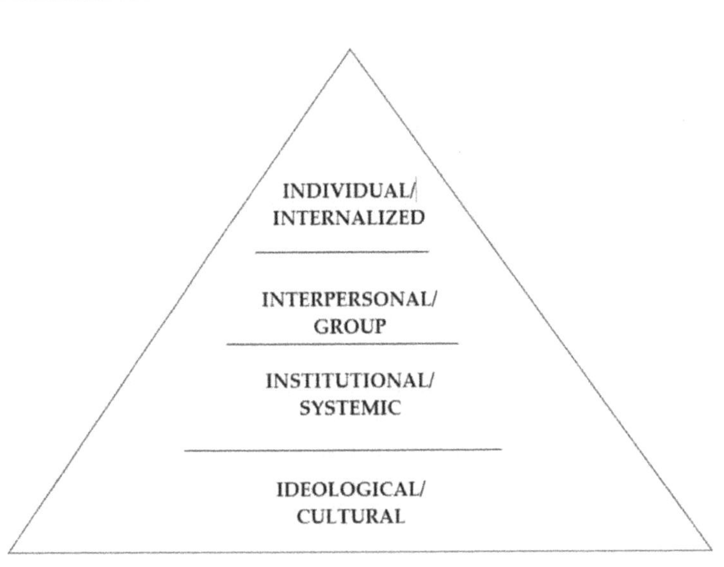

These levels operate intentionally and unintentionally, consciously and unconsciously.

The First is Ideological Oppression. *I learned that this country has at its core the idea that White people are somehow better than all people of color and that they, the white people, have the* *right to control people of color. This belief is described in the many ways that White people are described- more intelligent, harder working, stronger, capable, noble, deserving, advanced, chosen, normal, superior, and so on.*

In conjunction with this idea that White people hold about themselves, they also attribute opposite or contrasting qualities to People of Color: stupid, lazy, weak, incompetent, worthless, less deserving, backward, abnormal, inferior, and so on. Interestingly, this also became clear when studying the culture of Trinidad and Tobago as the same positive and negative attributes are used in the same oppressive ways.

In taking an inventory of the ideas that were taught to me as a child in my home, school, and church, it supported the better than another way of thinking. The ideology of the dominant group in power is one that tries to define for everyone what their 5C's of identity should and must be. They set up cultural norms imposed on others, and often internalized.

The Second is Institutional Oppression. *The colonial idea that one group is better than another group and has the right to control the other was, and still is, embedded in the institutions of society both in Trinidad and Tobago and the*

United States - laws, the legal system and police practices, the education system and schools, hiring policies, public policies, housing developments, media images, political power, etc.

When a woman makes two-thirds of what a man makes in the same job, it is institutionalized sexism. Here in the United States, when one out of every four African American young men is currently in jail, on parole, or on probation, it is institutionalized racism.

When psychiatric institutions and associations "diagnose"

transgender people as having a mental disorder, it is institution-alized gender oppression and transphobia. Institutional oppression does not have to be intentional. For example, if a policy unintentionally reinforces and creates new inequalities between privileged and non-privileged groups, it is still institutional oppression.

Awareness will hopefully lead to transformation. By this, I mean becoming aware of one's 5C's of Identity should lead to the process of the 5C's of Transformation. I want to offer the difference between transformation and change. Change is temporary, like we change our clothes or even change our physical appearance. Transformation is permanent. It is like the transformation of a butterfly.

A caterpillar must go through a painful and lonely time in its life (the period spent in its cocoon) to transform into a beautiful butterfly. Although getting to this final stage is not an effortless process, every step of that process is necessary. When the transformation is complete, there is no turning back.

The third is Interpersonal Oppression. *The idea that one group is better than another and has the right to control the other has become incorporated into institutions. This type of oppression involves permission and reinforcement by institutions for individual members of the dominant group to disrespect or mistreat individuals in the oppressed group personally.*

Interpersonal racism is what white people do to people of color up close--the racist jokes, the stereotypes, the beatings and harassment, the threats, micro-aggressions etc. Similarly, interpersonal sexism is what men do to women-- the sexual abuse and harassment, the violence directed at women, the belittling or ignoring of women's thinking, the sexist jokes, etc. Most people in the dominant group are not consciously oppressive. They have internalized the negative messages about other groups and consider their attitudes toward the other groups quite normal.

There is no such thing in the U.S. culture as "reverse racism," "reverse sexism," "reverse adultism," etc. While the oppression of minority groups is backed up in this country by the power of institutional arrangements, when the oppressed people act harmfully, they have no power behind them. The issue of power is an important one here.

People of Color, women, and youth can have prejudices against and anger toward individual White people (in connection with racism), men (in connection with sexism), and adults (in connection with adultism). They can act out those feelings in destructive and hurtful ways toward Whites, men, and adults. But in every case, this act will be severely punished. The force of the police and the courts, or at least a gang of whites getting even, will come crashing down on those people. The individual prejudice of Black people, for example, is not accepted by the legal system and prevailing white institutions.

The oppressed group, therefore, does not have the power to enforce its prejudices, unlike the dominant group. For example, the racist and public killing of George Floyd and countless killings of unarmed Black bodies are carried out every day by racist sanction institutional police departments and upheld by a racist criminal justice system.

*This would not have happened if Floyd and other Black men had been White and the officers, Black. A simple definition of racism, as a system, is **RACISM = PREJUDICE + POWER.** Therefore, with this definition of the systemic nature of racism, People of Color cannot be racists. The same formula holds true for all forms of oppression. The dominant group has its mistreatment of the target group embedded in and backed up by society's institutions and other forms of power.*

The Fourth is Internalized Oppression. *One especially important* *awareness that I came to as I studied oppression involved the way oppression works <u>within</u> the oppressed groups of people. Oppressed people internalize the ideology of inferiority. They see it reflected in the institutions in their communities; they experience disrespect interpersonally from members of the dominant group; and they eventually come to internalize the negative messages about themselves.*

People of color have been told they are stupid, worthless, abnormal, and have been treated as if we were unworthy of respect and appreciation, so it is not surprising that we would come to believe it.

This makes us feel bad. Oppression always begins from outside the oppressed group, but by the time it gets internalized, the external oppression hardly be felt because the damage has already been done.

If people from the oppressed group feel bad about themselves and, because of the nature of the system, do not have the power to direct those feelings back toward the dominant group without receiving more blows, then there are only two places to dump those feelings of oneself and the people in the same group or a still more oppressed and devalued group. This has been the case with poor Whites who see minorities as the problem. "Thus, people in any target group must struggle hard to avoid feeling heavy feelings of powerlessness or despair." They often tend to put themselves and others down in ways that mirror the oppressive messages they have gotten all their lives").

Acting out internalized oppression runs the gamut from passive powerlessness to violent aggression. If the accepted norm is white and any deviation is seen as less important or even worthless, then internalized oppression is the result. The media presented me, even while I was in Trinidad, with countless examples of the "nor-mal" and "White" being the norm, "normal," "human," and all "oth-ers" as "abnormal," "nonhuman." Like all children growing up in Trinidad and Tobago, this is why I wanted to be Tarzan, the Lone Ranger, or one of the Brady Bunch. Watching those shows in Trinidad and now constantly seeing these images in United States media and advertising has resulted in my internalizing what I now understand to be racism or White Supremacy. In other words, to be American = White = Human. Whether it is schools, media, church, and even your own home, if we learn to accept this formula and with an ardent desire to try to fit this formula, it is not surprising that even today after having had a Black President, we, People of Color, still try to be White, inwardly, and outwardly.

This leads us to love the things that White people love and hate the things they hate, which include People of Color. Hence, we find ourselves suffering from self-hatred and internalized racism. This internalization is at the root of the prevalent practice of referring to oneself or members of the same ethnic group using racially derogatory terms such as "nigga" "Dawg" "Mother Fucker" and "Cunt." We decided that this is acceptable because it stays within the self or group and does not offend any outsiders. When I ask People of color, especially those who identify themselves as Black, why they take part in these types of behaviors, they present a variety of reasons. For example, one justification is that they want to put themselves down before someone else tries to. Some say they are trying to fight against the harmful nature of these terms by using them as endearing ones with their closest family and friends.

Some are now so comfortable with these terms that they do not see any reason to stop using them. All these explanations come from hating and rejecting your C's of Color because everyone around you does the same to you. It is giving in and joining in the continuation of racism and White Supremacy that happens in the culture and context around us. And again, it becomes internalized. It was also very important for me to understand that the internalized patterns of racist thinking and behavior originally developed unconsciously and even consciously, was a way to keep people alive because, at that time to speak and reject them openly would lead to expulsion from one's family, church, school, work, and social group. The sad reality is that some of us still today see them as having survival value in a world where we are all trying to just live.

SUMMARY OF THE 4I's OF OPPRESSION:

INDIVIDUAL (INTERNALIZED):

Attitudes and beliefs we come to believe are true about ourselves and others through social socialization.

INTERPERSONAL (GROUP):

Our patterns of interactions and behaviors with other people that are taught to us through institutions and are supported by the family, the peer group, and the community.

INSTITUTIONAL (SYSTEMIC):

The systemic basis by which resources and power are controlled by the dominant group in society through institutional policies and practices, which are both conscious and unconscious, intentional and unintentional.

IDEOLOGICAL (CULTURAL):

The assumptions, beliefs, messages, and symbols that reinforce aesthetic, behavioral qualities, and norms as beautiful, right, and good, and the assumption that deviations from those norms are somehow unacceptable, inappropriate, and/or inferior.

ENDING OPPRESSION:

I realize that the only way we can end institutional oppression is that each one of us, individually and collectively as members of an oppressed group (I=We), must undo the internalized beliefs, attitudes, and behaviors that stem from the oppression. We must create unity in the group, support its leaders, feel proud of its history, contributions, and potential, develop the strength to challenge patterns that hold the group back, and organize our group into an effective force for social change.

Internalized Privilege is another context in which White people need to acknowledge and change. They are people who benefit the most from these systems of oppression and internalize privilege. Privileged people involuntarily accept stereotypes and false assumptions about oppressed groups made by the dominant culture. Internalized privilege includes an acceptance of a belief in the inherent inferiority of the oppressed group and the inherent superiority or normalcy of one's own privileged group. Internalized privilege creates an unearned sense of entitlement in members of the privileged group and can be expressed as a denial of the existence of oppression and as white male paternalism.

The "4I's" is an interrelated system. It should be clear that none of these four aspects of oppression can exist separately. It is crucial to see any oppression as a system of oppression. It should also be clear that trying to challenge oppression in any of the four aspects will affect the other three.

The 10 C's Model of Identity Awareness and Transformational Change

© 2003 Ulric Johnson and Patti DeRosa

The "10C's" is a two-part model that includes the 5C's of Identity Awareness and the 5C's of Transformational Change. The 5C's of Identity Awareness are: Color, Culture, Class, Character, and Context. The 5C's of Transformational Change are: Confidence, Courage, Commitment, Conflict, and Community. In the 10C's Model, each of these words is used both literally and symbolically to be a variety of concepts under each theme.

The many identities with which I described myself earlier are all a part of my 10C's. Each gives information about who I am, my life history, different experiences, how I perceive myself, and how others perceive me in this country and the world. They tell part of the story of my life, yet no words or labels can accurately capture the totality of who we truly are. The 10C's is an attempt to bring together as many parts of the whole as possible. Each of the 10C's are interrelated. None can stand alone, and neither developed in isolation from the rest.

We must start with an inventory of ourselves and examine our own experiences to confront issues of personal and societal oppression more effectively. This self-inventory is an essential first step in the long journey toward social change. By recognizing our experiences as oppressors and as oppressed and by empathizing with the experiences of others, we begin moving toward social justice. The purpose, however, is not solely for self-exploration.

A deep level of self-knowledge can lead us to act to challenge oppression both personally and systemically. Understanding one's own 10C's moves us toward healing the wounds of isolation that result from the fragmentation of our identities in an oppressive society.

This fragmentation has caused us to lose sight of the richness and beauty of the diversity within and around us. Exploration of the 10C's can give us insight into the positive resources and hidden talents we each have and provide us with renewed energy to transform all forms of oppression we confront daily.

The 10C's is an attempt to move from the individualistic ideology of I=I to the more collective philosophy of I=we, thereby replacing the all-too-familiar "win-lose" and "better than" mentalities. It sees difference as an asset and a resource, not a problem. What follows is a description of each element of the 10C's Model.

The 10 C's of Identity Awareness: Color, Culture, Class, Character, and Context

The first "C" is Color. *The word "color," refers to individual/group identity based on the color of one's skin and "race" that is either self-determined or defined by those in power.*

In the "C" of Color, the word color is used primarily in a very literal sense to mean only skin color (not race per se). As "race" is a socially constructed concept, the model should place it in the second "C" of Culture, which ascribes meaning and definition to our identities and our worlds. However, because race functions as if it were "real," it can be included in the first "C" of Color as well.

This "C" is also used symbolically to mean all aspects of the self/group that are a part of one's core identity or essence, especially attributes such as color, sex, sexual orientation, and physical appearance and abilities.

This "C" includes other aspects of identity such as religion (being Buddhist) and ethnicity (being Chinese), but here we use them only as descriptions. The social meaning of these descriptions will be discussed in the next "C" of Culture. This first "C" of Color is a simple statement of description that is not yet value laden.

Color blindness, as a means of avoiding discussing race, is still very much practiced in personal, professional, and political contexts. The country elected its first President of color and had a family of color for two terms in the "White House." However, color, race, and racism continue to be overly sensitive topics that even people of color do not understand, want to understand, or about which they want to engage in continued dialogue.

We seem to dance around the impact the "C" of Color has on the culture and all aspects of relationships within home, school, or church. It is the one "C" of identity that most people continue to ignore, even when I give presentations, workshops, or training on race. I honestly believe that until we stop avoiding the reality of race, a social construct designed to promote white supremacy, this country and the world will continue the oppression of People of Color.

The second "C" is Culture. *The term culture means the values, beliefs, symbols, behaviors, ways of living, and shared history of a group of people (that may or may not belong to the same ethnic, racial, or gender groups). The ways in which a culture is shared and continually changes and are passed on from one generation to the next. The word Culture in this book is meant to incorporate all the above, with a special focus on the way that culture decides meaning, interpretations, and definitions. Culture interprets the meaning of the other "C's" of Color, Character, Class, and Context.*

For example, the physical color of one's skin "just is," but culture and context define certain skin. Colors as different

"races" and assign them either positive or negative values.

Because of varying cultural definitions, a person who is considered white in one culture may be defined as a person of color in another culture.

The terms male and female describe physical anatomy (sex), but culture tells us what it means to be male or female. Culture creates the concept of gender and defines proper gender roles. Therefore, sex and skin color are part of the first "C" of Color, but gender and race fall under the second "C" of Culture, as they are socially constructed categories that change from culture to culture.

The gender identity of whom is seen as male or female stays consistent among cultures (although even this assumption is more complex than it first appears) but the gender roles and behaviors expected of each sex will vary from culture to culture. Men may be allowed to show physical affection toward each other in one culture but be discouraged from doing so in another culture.

A woman may weigh 200 pounds (a description, and therefore part of the "C" of Color) and be seen as beautiful in one culture yet be seen as unattractive in another. Hair offers us another concrete example of these concepts. Hair just is - it is neither good nor bad. Culture (and specifically racist culture) defines European-type hair as "good" and African-type hair as "bad."

All cultures have both positive and negative aspects. I love being Trinbagonian. I love the sounds of the language, the rhythms of Calypso and Soca music, the tastes and smells of the food, and the sense of community and history. But Trinidad and Tobago are still a culture with extreme elements of sexism, adultism, and internalized racism. These are viewed as "traditional" practices and even accepted as normative cultural behavior. This is reflected in the substantial number of homicides, domestic violence, and child abuse that are reported and reflected daily the Trinidadian media. The lack of laws, and the failure to enforce those that are set up, is another example of institutionalized and internalized isms.

This is true for each of our cultures. No culture is free of oppression, and we must be courageous enough to name it and challenge it wherever it exists. Sexism and heterosexism are two forms of oppression that are often excused under the guise of culture, tradition, and religion. I strongly challenge this notion, and I believe that any attitude or behavior that hurts, limits, or devalues another human being is oppressive, whether it is accepted cultural practice or not.

The third "C" is Class *and addresses power relations. It examines* *individual and group identity compared to power, authority, hierarchy, status, and the degree of access to, control over, or ownership of resources, including wealth, education, employment, housing, etc. The first "C" of Color describes us, the second "C" of Culture defines and categorizes us, and this third "C" of Class positions and places us in the social structure.*

This "C" of Class is used in a much broader sense than economic class alone to talk about power and privilege in psychological and material ways. For example, white people experience privilege in a racist society based on white supremacy even if they do not have economic power. Men have power over women in a sexist society even as they may experience other forms of oppression such as racism and heterosexism.

The issue of power is critical and still often stays unacknowledged in discussions about individual and group identity. This continued failure to recognize power imbalances is a key obstacle to productive and authentic dialogue about diversity because it avoids the fundamental issues of access, ownership, and control over one's own/group's life.

Without the notion of power differences, diversity education stays at the level of valuing differences and avoids the more challenging work of identifying and challenging "isms." Personal prejudice must not be confused with the systemic institutionalization of prejudice by those who have dominant group power in a society.

We all have power. Some of that power is personal, some is institutional, and some is historical. The discussion of power is not intended to place blame nor to induce guilt, although these feelings may be generated when discussing the use and misuse of power. The goal is to find and accept the power that we do have and to creatively use that power in the service of social justice. Denial of the social realities that shape our lives blocks our efforts toward recognition of oppression and undermines our ability to produce true social change.

Many of us live on both sides of the power line. As a Black man, I experience oppression daily because of my race, yet I experience some privilege compared to my gender. A White heterosexual female will experience oppression as a woman yet also receives help from white skin privilege. We both experience heterosexual privilege. Yet we all have the obligation to use whatever power we have in ways that work for peace and justice.

The fourth "C" is Character*. Character refers to the unique aspects of each individual person, including personal preferences, idiosyncrasies, and personality traits. People who share similar color, culture, class, and context still have aspects of the self that are unique to the individual. For example, my brother and I are identical twins.*

I share the same Color, Culture, and Class as my twin brother, Eric, but we are still unique and separate individuals. Steven, who I worked very closely with, doing antiracism work, is a White American male who shares many common experiences with other White American males, yet he has unique characteristics that distinguish him and make him special.

In many diversity programs, diversity is defined primarily as individual uniqueness. While it is true that diversity includes individual uniqueness, this definition ignores the importance of group identity and inadvertently reinforces the Eurocentric notion of "we are all individuals."

It also ignores the power differentials between groups that lead to the inclusion of some and the exclusion of others.

When you are a member of a dominant group in society (i.e. White, male, Christian, etc.), your first three "C's" of Color, Culture, and Class are continually confirmed for you every day in the media, in schools, and in every other setting.

In other words, dominant group members' identities are supported and reflected everywhere, so that they become invisible. They appear to be "the norm" or "the standard." When your "group identities" of Color, Culture, and Class are confirmed at every turn, your area of focus then becomes your individuality. You become blind to the other identities that often right in front of you. What this means is that you rarely think about these aspects of your identity. If you are White, you may think of People of Color as having a race or culture, but somehow think of yourself as "neutral."

It should not be a surprise that dominant group members most often tend to place their focus on their "C" of Character. I often hear this repeatedly in workshops. I also hear it daily in the news, when we talk about how President Obama, was treated, compared to President Trump, how the concerns about "Black Lives Matter," compared to the "Me-too" movement.

White people will say: "Why do we have to talk about race? Why can't we all just be individuals? I don't think of myself as having a race." For People of Color, whose Color, Culture, and Class are constantly either under attack, excluded, or distorted, the response is just the opposite.

From them, we hear, "I have to focus on my group's identities until you finally see, acknowledge, and respect me. The stereotyping of my group identities strips away my individuality."

Personal identities and social group identities are equally important, and the exclusion or minimization of either leads to internal and external conflict and a distortion of reality. It is also important to remember that our character is not formed in isolation. Our indi-

viduality is shaped by the social conditions of our C's of Color, Culture, Class, and Context.

The Fifth "C" of Context *is the reality in which individuals and groups exist in time, location, environment, and the sociopolitical, economic, and historical conditions that influence individual and group experience. Color, Culture, Class, and Character cannot be seen in isolation from context and cannot be fully understood when removed from the context that shapes their meaning.*

I often conduct training with human service workers or with teachers of color. In these contexts, my identity as a Person of Color is often affirmed, and as a result, I feel freer to be myself. Yet, when I do corporate training, there may be few, if any, People of Color in the room. Since I am a person of color myself, this aspect of my "C's" is noticeably clear. My race stands out and is, in fact, often challenged usually by the White male participants.

White people often experience this same dynamic when they are the only White people in the room. We have all had the experience of feeling more relaxed and more truly ourselves when with friends and family than when we are with strangers or at work. In environments that are familiar and in which we feel valued, we do not feel the need to check any part of ourselves at the door to be accepted.

Context means that our identities take on a different significance depending on where we are, who we are with, and the political realities of the moment. Think back to my story of being a 13-year-old coming to the United States in 1973. In the context of Trinidad, my style of speech "just was" (the first "C" of Color), and within the Trinidadian culture, it was seen as normative. In the culture and context of the United States, however, I was suddenly perceived as having an "accent," which was seen as a negative trait, and after I became self-conscious about something that I never had to think about before.

Context can also be historical. Being Jewish in Germany in the 1930s and 1940s has different nuances of meaning than being Jewish in the 21st century in the United States, although both experiences are deeply connected. Being of African heritage in the United States does not mean the same thing as being of that same heritage in Europe.

This idea of context can help us get past the destructive tendency to compare oppressions and place them in a hierarchy. The context will decide which oppression should have priority at any moment. This approach tries to address immediate social conditions without minimizing or devaluing the pain caused by any one oppression. Context is fluid, not static. Various aspects of our "C's" will rise to the surface and take precedence in different contexts. Context is like the basket that holds the other C's together.

To summarize:

Color describes and finds, Culture explains and gives meaning, Class ranks and positions, Character distinguishes and names uniqueness, and Context impacts and shapes.

The 5 C's of Transformational Change: Confidence, Courage, Commitment, Conflict, and Community

Once we have found, explored, and accepted our 5C's of Identity Awareness, we must put this awareness to use. Our challenge is how to put this awareness to use within a context that continues to devalue and fragment these aspects of our identities and perpetuate oppression.

There are certain elements that can help us move toward activism and empower us to work for a peaceful, just, and humane society, and the 5C's of Change try to supply a roadmap. Just as in our 5C's of Identity Awareness, there may be aspects of our 5C's of Change that we readily acknowledge and embrace and others that we deny or are unaware of. Again, the first step is to do a self-inventory to find strengths and areas in need of improvement and growth.

The First "C" of Change is (building) Confidence. *Confidence is faith in yourself and in your abilities. It is the belief that you can make a difference alone and with other people. To have true confidence, you must understand and take pride in all aspects of your 5 C's of Awareness, including race, ethnicity, gender, class, and sexual orientation.*

Reclaiming and redefining one's personal and group identities and abilities in ways that are inclusive of all people will build confidence and unleash creativity that can enrich and enhance the quality of life for all people.

The Second "C" of Change is (inspiring) Courage. *Courage is the* *ability to act despite fear. We've all heard the myth of the "fear-less leader," but leaders are never truly fearless. What leaders do is act despite the fear they may have and use it to motivate themselves.*

Courage means acting as a leader and being willing to take the risks that leadership demands. Dr. Martin Luther King, Jr. defined courage as "the inner resolution to go forward in spite of obstacles and frightening situations." ("Martin Luther King, Jr. on Fear – The Imperfectionist"). His wisdom can guide and nourish us in difficult political times of backlash against movements for peace and social justice.

The Third Element of the 5C's of Change is (sustaining) Commitment. *We define Commitment as focus, strategy, determination, and consistency, driven by love and grounded in knowledge. By love, we mean the deep and consistent passion for justice and the embrace of humanity that has always driven social revolutions.*

By knowledge, we mean correct education about history and culture that includes multiple perspectives, especially those whose stories have been silenced. But passion without knowledge can become dangerous and reckless, and knowledge without passion can become stilted, intellectualized posturing that is divorced from activism. True commitment must incorporate both elements.

The Fourth Element of the 5C's of Change is (engaging in) Conflict. *This refers to the reflection, struggle, and creative tension that promote growth and justice. Conflict is a positive and necessary part of the process of change. Conflict is often defined as negative, but when channeled appropriately, it is a force that can propel us forward.*

Like the avoidance of the issue of power, avoidance of conflict is often used as a means of preventing us from challenging injustice. Like power, conflict also often brings up feelings and images of blame and guilt. But conflict is just the meeting of opposing ideas that can lead to a win-win solution rather than the win-lose scenario presented by the dominant culture as the only outcome. Conflict moves us toward our "growing edge." We need to examine our own conflict styles and their relationship to our use of power. Do we avoid conflict? Do we incite conflict? Are we inspired by conflict? Do we fear conflict? These are questions that must be considered as we move toward activism and work for justice.

The Final "C" of the 5C's of Change is (co-creating) Community. *Community means working collectively and collaboratively with others toward a shared vision that acknowledges, values and affirms human diversity as essential to the individual, as well as to the whole (**I=We and We=I**). A support system is an essential element of building a peaceful and just society. We cannot do this work alone. A support system that is inclusive of diverse people and points of view provides us with a richer sense of ideas and possibilities of which we would otherwise not be conscious. We believe that Community means valuing not only your own 10C's but the 10C's of others as well.*

Being surrounded and supported by a loving and affirming community helps to build confidence, courage, commitment, and the ability to deal with conflict. Community helps us to see and connect with our allies, gives us encouragement, and sustains us through challenging times of struggle.

Summary of the 10C's Model:

The 10C's model is flexible and has grown and changed along with those of us who have used it. A "4C's Model," which included Color, Culture, Class, and Context, was originally developed by me in the early 1980s to help me explain my experiences as an Afro-

Trinidadian in the United States. At that time, I used the words quite literally. It was only later that, together Patti and I added more "C's" and came to see how the model could be used to explore a wide range of identity issues.

We both believe that this adaptability makes the model applicable cross-culturally and across age ranges (youth to adults) as it integrates cultural as well as developmental perspectives. The "C" of Context makes the model flexible enough to take into consideration historical as well as present-day realities.

The 10C's bless us with the opportunity to see and experience the power of dialogue to promote change. We bear witness to people as they experience a sense of what is possible, for if they can create an authentic experience in the workshop or classroom, they can replicate it elsewhere in their lives. A model is only an intellectual tool. It comes alive when we act on the new awareness and knowledge we have gained and use the tools and skills we have learned in creative ways. A hammer in a toolbox will never build a house until someone picks it up! The 10C's can be thought of as a blueprint for a new house. Let the building begin!

10 C's FOCUSED COUNSELING

10C's Focused Counseling is a multicultural process of counseling individuals in Reconnecting, Reclaiming, Redefining, and Celebrating all aspects of their Identity by becoming Aware and Transforming how they relate to their 10C's and those of others. I use it in my work as an Antiracism Educator, Consultant, Coach, Mental Health Counselor, and Marriage and Family Therapist, primarily working with Clients of Color.

It is based on the awareness and transformational process I personally went through and continues daily. The goal is to help clients become proficient in the awareness of their 10C's.

The three key focus areas of awareness and transformational change that I went through are adjusting my attitudes and increasing my knowledge and skills necessary to address the internalized negative beliefs about my 10C's due to past traumatic experiences due to racism. I had to first redefine my 5 C's of Identity: Color, Culture, Class, Character, and Context, and the second 5C's of Transformational Change: Confidence, Courage, Committeemen, Conflict, and Community.

*I believe that first going through the process helped me better help my clients (individual, couples, group, organization etc..) develop an awareness of their own 10C's. This must be grounded in the ideology and process of genuine LOVE (**LOVE: L**isten- **O**pen - **V**ulnerable - **E**mphatic), of each other's 10C's, and understanding their interconnectedness with how they Think, Feel and Behave (total behavior) during the counseling process.*

The lack of awareness of a client's multicultural and diverse set of beliefs and practices could prevent both you and the client from developing a more genuine relationship. The key to developing a relationship of trust is showing a genuine interest in learning, understanding, and incorporating the cultural beliefs and practices used by the client to address mental health issues caused by past traumas.

I believe that an antiracist counselor must be proficient in helping Clients of Color to value their own diversity, conduct ongoing self-assessments, manage the daily dynamics of different relationships, as well as cultural contexts.

Learn to become proficient in combining Internal and External awareness of your 10C's. Both the clinician and client must work from an attitude of openness and seek ways to explore their own 10C's perspectives and biases. This ability to keep an interpersonal relationship that is oriented in looking to understand the other, and at the same time being understanding once self is referred to as an I=We counseling relationship.

Focus Areas of Client Identity Self - Transformation

BELIEFS – ATTITUDES

Focus on clients' <u>awareness</u> of and <u>sensitivity</u> to their own 10C's.

Focus on clients' <u>awareness</u> of their values and biases and how they may affect their relationships to self, family, community, and general society.

Focus on clients' level of <u>sensitivity to circumstances</u> (personal biases, stage of identity development, sociopolitical influences, etc.) and how they go about their daily lives.

Focus on clients' awareness and ability to be <u>flexible and</u> <u>open</u> to new knowledge of self and others.

Focus on clients' <u>ability to cope and manage</u> the effects of past personal, interpersonal, institutional, social, and cultural trauma due to his/her 5C's of Identity.

KNOWLEDGE

Focus on helping clients develop an <u>understanding</u> of the sociopolitical system of the United States and its <u>implications</u> for majority and minority groups.

Focus on helping clients become <u>aware</u> of the institutional barriers and how to navigate them.

the obstacles that often prevent clients of color from using health and mental health services.

Focus on helping clients <u>develop a clear and explicit knowledge</u> <u>and understanding</u> of the generic characteristics of mental health counseling and therapy.

Focus on helping clients <u>develop a clear and explicit knowledge and understanding</u> of the generic characteristics of collaborative leadership.

Focus on helping clients <u>develop a clear and explicit knowledge and understanding</u> of a violent lifestyle versus a non-violent lifestyle (violence: anything a person chooses to do, unconsciously or consciously, to hurt oneself or another person or thing).

<u>SKILLS</u>

I focus on helping clients generate a wide variety of nonviolent verbal and nonverbal responses to personal, interpersonal, professional, and social conflict.

Focus on helping clients to be able to <u>send and receive both</u> verbal and nonverbal messages accurately and appropriately.

Focus on helping clients use their awareness of cultural, institutional, and systemic policies to advocate for themselves and others when appropriate.

*Focus on helping clients to be able to generate a variety of ways to <u>LOVE and respond to being LOVED. (**LOVE: L**isten- **O**pen - **V**ulnerable - **E**mphatic)</u>*

Focus on helping clients to be able to generate a variety of ways to have fun, a sense of control, a sense of safety, <u>and helping others to do the same.</u>

Part Four of the Journey: The Five Stages of 10C's FOCUS COUNSELING

*Stage I: **L**istening and attending to 10 C's (Content – Feeling and Meaning)*

*Stage II: **O**pen to unlearn - relearn – learn.*

*Stage III: **V**ulnerable to taking risks.*

*Stage IV: **E**mphatic relationships*

Stage One: Listening

*The counseling process begins with listening, with the clinician being present with genuine compassion for the client. Creating a safe space for them to share their concerns, issues, thoughts, and feelings from the perspective of their 10C's **Goals of Stage I:***

Encouraging the client to "get it out," being transparent, honest, and authentic in expressions of their thoughts, feelings, and needs provides an opportunity for the client to experience being heard and that their C's are valued. Clarify and sort out needs from the client's C's perspective they want to address.

Objectives of Stage I:

Create a safe, trusting, and respectful context for sharing by listening, listening, listening.

To share aspects of one's 10Cs and role model awareness and value, establish the foundation of working with and doing with, and Identify areas of strength, knowledge, and skills.

Due to intergenerational trauma caused by institutional and systemic "ism-s," most people strongly need to be heard. The client's experience of being truly listened to can be all they may need. Sometimes they simply need to hear themselves talk as they join someone in a space that is considered safe and peaceful.

"Thank you for listening to me. I have been in and out of counseling for over ten years, and it is only…"

Now that I feel that someone has truly listened to me. You somehow made the connection between how I feel about my color, culture, and country and how I feel about myself. Yes, there are some bad things, but I now realize there are also a whole lot of good things."

35-year-old Black male from the Caribbean, seen for Major Depression.

Stage II OPENING: Unlearn-Relearn-Learn

All clients have the internal resources to address the many issues they bring to counseling sessions. With 10 C's Focus Counseling, our goal is to aid the client in being open to exploring these inner resources. Awareness of these inner resources leads to a place of self-empowerment and accepting responsibility for the choices made and being made. The process of unlearning, relearning, and learning about one's C's often creates a transformational - change that can be dramatic and instantaneous in how a client thinks, feels, and behaves.

Goals of Stage II:

Creating deeper awareness of the client's own issues. Moving from a place of powerlessness to self–empowerment. Establishing insight on how misinformation and the internalization of this information have limited their beliefs, feelings, and their abilities to solve their own problems.

Help clients understand what they rely on need, which may differ from what they believe is the problem. Set realistic goals to address the problem.

Objectives of Stage II*: Confronting ambivalence about the following:*

Awareness of one's 10C's. Exploration and reexamination of formed core values and beliefs.

Taking responsibility for choices made in the past and present.

The movement from a place of powerlessness to self-empowerment can often lead to feelings of being vulnerable and alone as the client adjusts to their newly found identity. The empowering process often leads people of color to realize they are not White and will not be accepted as White. The desire to be accepted by White society has often caused People of Color to adopt White ideology and ways of living.

This has often led to disappointment and anger. This anger can often lead to depression and anxiety which is a reaction to the disappointment in them for doing so in the first place. This new awareness often causes the client to end all association with White ideology or people, and they immerse themselves in learning more about their C's of identity, people, and history.

This is an overly sensitive process that requires a high degree of skill in guiding the client in redirecting their anger and disappointment from individuals and their own social identity group to systems and institutions that promote isms.

"I have come to understand that what I was told I need to be successful, a house, car, money, college education, is all a lie. That my being alive, healthy, intelligent, and loving myself is what

being successful is all about. I am disappointed and angry that I have been lied to and spent 45 years of my life pursuing something that took time and energy that I could have used to appreciate me. But it's better late than never."

45-year-old Black African American female graduate student, seen Major Anxiety and Depression.

Stage III: Vulnerable - Taking Risks

As the client becomes aware of their inner resources, the counselor helps the client explore their feelings of being vulnerable due to new awareness of their C's. This transformational process of new knowledge means that one must now take risks in being honest by taking responsibility for their own thinking, feelings, and behaviors.

Goals of Stage III:

Generate options for the continued application of new ways of Thinking, Feeling, and Behaving. Redefining inner relationship with self and others. Development of inner courage and confidence in oneself.

Objectives of Stage III: Sharing ambivalence about the following:

1. Development of confidence in one's own C's

2. Developing the courage to act

3. Develop the ability to engage in conflict non-violently.

When the client has fully integrated their C's of Identity Awareness and actively engages in Identity Transformation, they are then ready to reestablish relationships with others from a place of empathy. With this new knowledge and awareness, the next step is putting it into action. This requires the client to develop new ways that they could collaborate with White people and their own people of color.

"Through coming to see you for counseling, I now realize that as a Black man, I have made a lot of mistakes in my relationships,

especially with women and that I need to not only change the way I think but the way I behave. I know I will lose a lot of my friends because of how I change, but I need to do this for me. I would just have to make new friends."

25-year-old Black African American male being seen for Anger Management.

Stage IV Empathy: New Ways of Relating

The 10C's Model requires people to act on their new awareness of the resources that come with their C's. Establishing new ways of relating in one's personal, professional, and political life, based on the foundation of empathy and respect for their own and others' C's. Working collaboratively with others to create communities that respect each other C's. This means consistent effort in looking at how systems and institutions prevent the building of "I=We" relationships.

Goals of Stage IV:

1. *Addressing Systemic Transformational change.*

2. *Examine the client's commitment to action steps.*

3. *Expect and address potential conflict and challenges.*

Objectives of Stage IV: Shared vision and collective action.

1. *Collective work for social justice and transformation in personal, professional, and political contexts. Creating context that can heal the remnants of racism and internalized 10C's oppression.*

2. *Encouraging critical thinking about community, country, and world*

The "I=We" process of 10C's Focus Counseling is to help People of Color realize their full potential individually and collectively. People of Color can never reclaim their power until they informally and formally accept accountability and responsibility for their choices and actions lovingly and effectively.

"One thing I learned from talking with you is that I must choose if I want to continue being part of the problem or part of the solution."

16-year-old Latino Latin King Gang involved male who now works to prevent gang violence.

Complementary but not always sequential:

The four-stage approach to the 10C's Focus Counseling is complementary, but not always sequential, to each other. If you and the client find that there is no movement in one stage, then you can move to the next stage, working on the goals and methods of that stage then go back to the earlier stage.

For example:

If the ability to Empathize (Stage IV) is not set up, go back to look at the client's ability to be vulnerable with self (Stage III).

If in Stage III, the client is having difficulty being vulnerable, go back to being open to unlearning, relearning, and learning new ways of Thinking, Feeling, and Behaving (Stage II).

If at any time the client feels the need to self-express, or we feel that a genuine relationship has not been set up, return to listening to the client while paying more attention to content, feeling, or meaning (Stage I).

Part Five of Journey: APPLYING THE 10 C'S MODEL

The 10C framework has helped many people in their personal development and shaped their work. It has proven useful to people in many fields, including teachers, administrators, parents, community workers, youth, and activists.

The model benefits individuals, groups, organizations, and communities by supplying simple and straightforward language for discussions about diversity and oppression in affirming and challenging ways. The 10C's approach acknowledges the existence of oppression and "isms" while simultaneously recognizing that oppression is learned behavior we can challenge and change by developing and mobilizing our talents and abilities.

The 10C's Model also helps us find areas of strength and those that need improvement.

We have used the model for both micro (individual, group, and therapeutic) and macro (organizations and systems) assessments. In the concluding section of this book, we offer some suggestions as to how to apply the model in various settings.

Youth and Community Work:

The model has had its clearest application in work with youth. Teens Against Gang Violence (TAGV) is a youth group rooted in a win/win ideology of peace and justice, with the 10C's serving as guidelines for personal development, group interactions, and community education. TAGV defines itself as a peace and justice gang formed by youth ages 12-20. The 10C's framework supplies a common language for TAGV and serves as an important foundation

for their activities. For example, members complete a "10C's In-
ventory," exploring their own personal and cultural resources.

*In their community work, the youth leaders use the framework to
talk with younger children. When problems arise in the group,
the 10C's serve as a guidepost for conflict resolution. Because the
framework emphasizes resources rather than deficits, it is a powerful alternative to the traditional win/lose ways in which society
defines youth. The model gives young people a positive language
for their own development.*

*The Women's Theological Center in Boston, MA, has successfully
used the 10C's Model in its work of developing transformational
spiritual leadership. They define spiritual or transformational leadership as that aspect of leadership that tends to relationships at all
levels – personal, interpersonal, institutional, and cultural, and that
creates and keeps environments that inspire growth and transformation to support individuals and collectives to live out their
deepest, most life-affirming values and purpose.*

Classroom Curriculum:

*The 10C's framework has contributed to several commercial and
teacher-made curricula for the past ten years. In collaboration with
William Kreidler of Educators for Social Responsibility (now Engaging Schools), the framework was applied to conflict resolution
curricula for elementary and middle school grades. Graduate students and teachers in our workshops have used the framework
to develop K-12 curricula in literature, social studies, science, and
the fine arts.*

*For example, a high school literature teacher uses the 10C's to
analyze the plot, character, and conflict in poetry and fiction, especially when exploring literature that deals with cultural conflict
and change. For her, the framework helps to shape classroom*

discussions, writing assignments, and final projects.

A primary school teacher uses the 10C's to shape the way cultural diversity is celebrated, and conflicts are resolved in her work with parents as well as children. In addition to classroom activities, the framework can help guide the way classroom teachers present, teach, and evaluate the outcome of their work, rather than measuring achievement simply through paper and pencil, win/lose tests. The framework opens evaluation to more holistic and culturally literate measures of change.

Counseling and Risk Prevention:

The issues and resources embedded in the 10C's framework have been helpful in structuring counseling groups for children, youth, families, and risk prevention programs. The 5C's of Awareness help group members explore their own identities and histories, name the contextual forces that may shape their behavior, and understand their differences and similarities. The 5C's of Change aid the group in examining the process of positive change and understanding as well as in supporting each other's journey.

Group activities can help develop and support members' confidence, courage, and commitment through an affirming approach to conflict that builds a sustainable sense of community within the group. The framework offers re-definitions for some traditional group dynamics, including race and gender, grief and loss, anger, and self-control.

More generally, the framework has been used to deepen prevention work in substance abuse, violence, and teen pregnancy. Color, culture, class, character, and context all shape how young people take risks, and which risks they choose to take. For example, if the community stereotypes young African American males as gang members, drug users, potential dropouts, and athletically but not *intellectually gifted, these young men are more likely to take certain kinds of risks and avoid others.*

They may seek validation for both their self-esteem and group esteem through confronting peers or dominating sexual relationships with young women rather than taking academically challenging courses or acting equitably in their sexual relations.

If the dominant culture defines beauty as light-skinned, thin, and sexually active, young women are likely to try to "prove" their worth by engaging in sexual relationships that are unsafe, both medically and psychologically, and prone to pregnancy and abuse.

The 10C's framework has helped young people, along with their teachers and counselors, to better understand the multiple factors that shape risky behavior, resulting in the development of the skills and relationships that help replace unhealthy risks with healthy ones. The framework reframes the very notion of risk, moving it from simplistic and ineffective "just say no" posturing to a method that recognizes how complex these decisions and actions really are. This approach empowers young people to think, act, and behave more responsibly.

Workplace Diversity and Systems Change:

The 10C's Model has been useful to adults seeking to change their own lives, workplaces, and Institutions. Businesses, health care, human services, and educational settings have found the model to be a powerful tool for both short-term and long-term interventions.

In public schools, educators are often painfully aware of the inequities in resources between different communities and the public policies that impact who graduates, who drops out, who secures sustainable employment, and who is marginalized. The 10C's framework has been a powerful lens and tool for teachers and administrators in this regard.

The 10C's Model has been an essential part of courses at Harvard University's Graduate School of Education, Lesley University's Master's degree program in Conflict Resolution, and Lesley University's annual Peaceable Schools Summer Institute help educators understand the problems and potential of public education and how to apply the 10C's Model to school change.

In addition to public sector and non-profit agencies, corporations and businesses have found the 10C's model an asset to their workplace diversity initiatives. A Fortune 500 company was experiencing higher than acceptable turnover, especially among women and People of Color. They were hiring and training good people, only to see too many leave too soon. Those who stayed with the company felt their talents and skills were undervalued and under-utilized.

This loss of talent translated into a big loss of dollars, and that was the wake-up call that led to their diversity initiative. After exposure to the 10C's Model in a leadership retreat, one of the executives said, "The key point for me was the importance of being open and listening and considering things from someone else's perspective, which adds a dimension to my own view. However, to really gain from understanding someone else's position, you must understand your own and know where you come from. The 10C's exercises showed me new elements of my identity that I had not considered before. Now I recognize common ground with people – grounds I could not see before."

Another said the training "gave us the tools to develop management techniques and skills for building a work climate that supports everybody reaching their full potential." The intensive training experience for these corporate leaders led them to commit to a long-term diversity initiative that reshaped the workplace climate, increased the number of women and people of color in key positions, and positively affected the bottom line.

The 10C's Model has helped to shift traditional diversity training and initiatives to a deeper, challenging commitment that includes concepts of social justice and equity. The framework helps expand the notion of diversity beyond valuing differences by encouraging the examination of issues of power, oppression, and liberation that are the heart of our society's diversity conflicts.

Although there are significant obstacles in any effort for institutional change, the 10C's Model has opened new doors for those who seek to transform their organizations.

The 10C's Model recognizes and celebrates complexity while at the same time supplying language with which to talk about difficult issues. It shifts our conversation from a win/lose, and a deficit approach to one that is win/win and asset based.

This Model sees difference as a resource, not a problem. Our own personal journeys of moving from seeing ourselves as defined by the dominant society to redefining our own identities on our own terms have helped us reshape how we do our work and how we live our lives.

Our work together as a Black male and White female continually demands us to "live the Model" as we experience the challenges and rewards of alliance building. We believe that all people can change, and we have lofty expectations that people will act on their increasing knowledge and awareness.

In fact, one workshop participant said quite spontaneously, "You actually expect us to do something with this!" We take comments like this as the highest form of praise.

Example One: 10C's of Self-Assessment

Please show the extent to which you agree or disagree with each of the following statements by using the codes listed below. Please give specific examples that support your assessment.

> **SA**   =Strongly Agree **A**= Agree **D** = Disagree **SD** =
>
> Strongly Disagree

Color: *I respect and appreciate my core individual and group identities.*

SA   A   D   SD

Culture: *I respect and appreciate my culture and values.*

SA   A   D   SD

Class: *I am aware of my individual power.*

SA   A   D   SD

Character: *I appreciate my own uniqueness as an individual.*

SA   A   D   SD

Context: *I am aware of how much my environment affects how I live.*

SA   A   D   SD

Confidence: *I am confident in being who I am.*

SA   A   D   SD

Courage: *I have the courage to stand up for myself.*

SA   A   D   SD

Commitment: *I am committed to doing whatever it takes.*

SA   A   D   SD

Conflict: *I can engage in conflict.*

SA   A   D   SD

Community: *I can work with others.*

SA   A   D   SD

10C's Self-Assessment Categories and Definitions

Color: *The ability to embrace and feel safe to show one's core individual and group identities. There is a feeling and expression of safety around learning about one's own identity and the identity of others. There is an open, honest, and authentic discussion about core identities.*

Culture: *The ability to be inclusive of all cultures and reflect a multicultural approach to addressing issues. Different languages and accents are used everywhere. Culture is not fixed and is subject to reflection and critique by all.*

Cultural differences are acknowledged, and their importance is neither denied nor belittled; hence, conflict is an acceptable part of the relations among people at all levels and is seen as an opportunity to gain experience and grow.

Class: *The ability to take on equal responsibility and ownership for decisions and their implementation. Representatives from all levels of the organization are accurately reflected on the decision-making council, board, and committees.*

Character: *The ability to address individual needs such as flexible schedules, interdisciplinary work, team teaching, mentoring, and accommodation of special needs.*

Context: *The ability to create environments and spaces that reflect the multiple identities of all who are involved. Learning is exciting, engrossing, inclusive, and evolving. Everyone is encouraged to take risks and challenge themselves by sharing their feelings and thoughts in addressing any issue affecting their or others' identities.*

Confidence: *The ability to express confidence in creating and influencing change. Feelings and language of hope are expressed about conflict at the personal and institutional level due to understanding and pride in their own and others' identities and histories. People can name other people they admire and respect because of their confidence in their own identity.*

Courage: *The ability to stand up for oneself and others and embrace the stories of leadership taken by people (individually and collectively) in frightening situations. To promote and keep peace and justice for all, regardless of their identities.*

Commitment: *The ability to be consistent in one's desire and seek out opportunities to learn about one's 10 C's, with the goal of how to best meet personal needs and the needs of others that promote peace and justice.*

There are continued individual and institutional strategies such as focus groups, community meetings, strategic planning retreats, and evaluation of all aspects and levels of the institution.

Conflict: *The ability to embrace and engage in addressing any conflict people may be experiencing regardless of their identities.*

Community: *The ability to work collectively and collaboratively. The attitude, feeling, and acknowledgment of "I = We" and "I have not made it unless WE all have made it." There is a lack of competition and more cooperation, even as they engage in conflict.*

Example Two:
10C's School/Community Organization Assessment

After reviewing the 5C's of the Awareness model, use this sheet to assess your school, community, or organization's status compared to its appreciation of its participants' 10C's.

Please show the extent to which you agree or disagree with each of the following statements by using the following codes. Please also give specific examples that support your assessment.

SA = Strongly agree   A= Agree   SD = Strongly disagree   D = Strongly disagree ("Effects of instrumental materials on student's academic … - GRIN")

Color*: Respect and appreciation for core individual and group identities.*

SA   A   SD   D

Individuals are encouraged and feel safe finding and showing their core individual and group identities. There is an open, honest, and authentic discussion about core identities.

Culture*: Respect and appreciation for diverse cultures and values.*

SA   A   SD   D

The activities include all cultures and reflect a multicultural approach to addressing issues. Different languages and accents are used everywhere. Culture is not fixed and is subject to reflection and critique by all.

Cultural differences are acknowledged, and their importance is neither denied nor belittled; hence, conflict is an acceptable part of the relations between people at all levels of the School/Community/Organization and is seen as an opportunity to gain experience and grow.

Class: *Differences in power are acknowledged by both individuals and the institution, and conscious efforts are made to include all, regardless of their 10 C's, in the decision-making process.*

SA   A   SD   D

Everyone has equal responsibility and ownership for decisions and their implementation. Representatives from all levels of the School/Community/Organization are accurately reflected on the decision-making counsel, board, and committees.

Character: *Individuals are recognized and appreciated for their unique talents and resources.*

SA   A   SD   D

Care is taken to address individual needs such as flexible schedules, interdisciplinary work, team teaching, mentoring, and accommodation of special needs.

Context: *The location is physically set up to welcome everyone's C's.*

SA   A   SD   D

The décor is one that reflects the 10C's of all who are involved. Learning is exciting, engrossing, inclusive, and evolving.

Everyone is encouraged to take risks and challenge themselves by sharing their feelings and thoughts in addressing any issues affecting their or others' 10C's. Signs welcome visitors and display core value statements. A diversity of people, regardless of their 5C's is seen all over and at various levels of the organization.

Confidence: *Understanding and taking pride in their 10C's.*

SA   A   SD   D

There is an expression of confidence in members to honestly influence change. Feelings and language of hope are expressed about conflict at the personal and institutional level due to understanding and pride in one's own and others' identities/histories. People can name others they admire and respect because of their confidence in their 10C's.

Courage: *The ability to take necessary action to promote peace and justice despite fear.*

SA   A   SD   D

Stories are told of leadership taken by people individually and collectively in frightening situations to promote and keep peace and justice for all, regardless of their 10C's. There are classes, presentations, and workshops on courage.

Commitment: *Expressed determination and consistency for non-violence, peace, and justice.*

SA   A   SD   D

There is a consistent desire to seek out opportunities to learn about one's 10C's, with the goal of how best to meet one's and others' needs that promote peace and justice. There is continued individual and institutional focus, with the help of strategies such as focus groups, community meetings, strategic planning retreats and evaluation of all aspects and levels of the institution.

Conflict: *The embracing of conflict as an opportunity to learn and grow.*

SA   A   SD   D

There are classroom meetings as well as community meetings to address any conflict that people may be experiencing. There is conflict mediation that is inclusive of everyone regardless of his or her 10C's. There are classes, presentations, and workshops on the nature of conflict and how it can be used to promote an appreciation of diversity, peace, and justice.

SA   A   SD   D

Community: *A shared vision that acknowledges, values, and affirms human ("Factors of Social Cohesion - 1304 Words - Internet Public Library") diversity as essential to the whole. ("Electronic Word Of Mouth Advantages And Disadvantages")*

SA   A   SD   D

There are examples of people working collectively and collaboratively, regardless of their 10C's. There is an attitude, a feeling and acknowledgement of I = We, that "I have not made it unless WE all have made it." There is lack of competition and more cooperation, even as they engage in conflict.

SA   A   SD   D

Example Three:
Circles of Power, Privilege, and Oppression

Goals:

- *Increase our understanding of socially constructed identity and how it is used in our society to assign value and rank in order to people to support systems of power and oppression.*

- *Explore the intersectionality of the multiple identities that everyone brings and increase our awareness of where we personally, professionally, and politically hold power or do not.*

- *Understand how issues of identity, privilege, power, and oppression play out and manifest themselves in our work relationships, especially as supervisors, supervisors, colleagues, and partners.*

Length: *about 2 hrs.*

Materials: 10C's Article, Flip Chart, Identity Circles worksheet

1. Looking at Identity: Identity Circles

A. *Introduce the concepts of the 10C's of Awareness and Change (DeRosa and Johnson, 2002.) To be true leaders for equity justice in schools, we must have a critical awareness of **who we are in relationship to others** – this involves taking an identity inventory of the multiple different identities we each have – what the authors call our First 5C's - **Color, Culture, Class, Character, and Context**.*

According to this model, we also need a second set of

*5C's - the **confidence** to stand for what we believe in, the **courage** to voice our opinions, a **commitment** to fairness and justice, a willingness to embrace **conflict**, and a **community** that encourages and supports our efforts.*

To actively work against racism and other systems of oppression in our schools and our communities, we must understand how OUR personal, professional, and political identities shape every interaction, action, decision, and choice we make.

B. *Using yourself as an example, share two of your own identities with the class (one where you are in the dominant group and one where you are in the minority or oppressed group). Find things about each identity that you feel good about.*

C. *Brainstorm identities on a flip chart.*

*The **5C's of Awareness— Color, Culture, Class, Character, and Context —** are the multiple identities we hold in the world, typically with varying degrees of awareness. Sometimes we see ourselves through our "primary" identity (I.e., gay/straight, female/male, POC/White, able-bodied, or differently abled).*

*To get at all these areas of identity, first have participants popcorn-style brainstorm all the different identities of which they can think. Often the easiest things for the group to think of will be **race, ethnicity, gender, age, class, ability, and religion.***

Invite participants to think more deeply by asking about more "invisible" identities such as sexuality, birth order, family role (sister/father), personality (comedian, introvert), cultural group, country of origin, languages, careers (boss, paper-pusher), hobbies, athletics, music/arts, neighborhoods, clubs, etc.... Remind participants of identities that are either sources of pride or stigma (mental illness, diabetes, cancer, or abuse survivors). Ask the group to share thoughts and opinions about the following:

- *Which identities can be changed?*

- *How does Context shape identity?*

- *Which identities are fixed and true for a lifespan?*

- *Within these categories, do certain identities give us power/advantage?*

- *Do certain identities disadvantage or disempower us?*

- *Which serve as sources of unearned oppression or privilege?*

D. *Hand out the "Identity Circles" Worksheets. Have participants take 5 minutes to reflect on their own multiple identities. Explain each of the identities/circles that are named (ethnicity/race, religion, gender, age, and class.) **NOTE:** Discussing "class" in particular, is often a challenge.*

Sometimes we talk about the poor, working class, middle class and wealthy or rich. But as we know, these labels can hold stigmas, and without extensive discussion, most people will most comfortably fill in the "middle class." It is helpful to define class as having access to money, material goods and resources (like education and healthcare). In this context, we can avoid the use of labels and instead ask participants to reflect on whether they think they feel they live with "enough," "not enough" or "more than enough" of those resources in their lives. It is important that participants feel they are the authorities over their own identities and that they can self-find without being corrected or judged by the facilitator or fellow participants.

E. *Ask participants to fill out the named circles with <u>what is</u> <u>true</u> <u>for them</u> (there can be more than one answer). Then ask them to fill in the unmarked circles with any identities they choose from the brainstormed list. Students can add identity circles if they want to.*

F. *Ask participants to reflect on their identities in each circle in terms of where they have experienced a source of power from that identity or have been disadvantaged or oppressed because of that identity. (Give an example from one of your own identities if this is unclear).*

G. *In pairs, triads, or foursomes, have participants take turns sharing at least two of their identity circles and a positive statement about each ("I am Puerto Rican, and Puerto Ricans are a strong people" ...I am the oldest child and I love being the boss." ... "I am a baseball player. I like being part of a team). Discuss the guiding questions raised earlier:*

- *Which of your identities has given you power/advantage?*

- *Which has disadvantaged or disempowered you?*

- *Where are your places of oppression, power, or privilege, and how do they intersect with others?*

- *How do these identities shape your personal/professional/political roles?*

H. *Large Group Debrief: Use the "Learned/Remembered/Wondered" method for debrief or simply popcorn share "one thing you heard/saw/felt" as you listened to and talked with your partners.*

2. Identity and Conflict

Ask participants now to think about the links between conflict and identity in their lives. Start off by having folks call out words that come to mind when you say the word "conflict" and record them all on flip chart paper. These first thoughts about conflict will often reflect negative feelings, responses, and actions. Ask them to think about a time when conflict in their life led to something positive. Take a minute to record their responses.

*Now ask them to take a moment, think back, and remember the last real conflict they had with someone else – **this was a teacher or a student, a friend or community partner, a sibling or parent, a funder or authority figure, an intimate partner or random stranger.** It happened recently or maybe long ago in the past. Ask them to share that conflict with a partner... share as many details as possible about who they were at the time of the conflict, what the context was, and the identity and context of the other person or party.*

What was the conflict about? Was it resolved, and how? Does any part of the conflict they describe seem rooted in or influenced by issues of their own or another person's identity? If yes, what about their identities in particular? How did histories and experiences of privilege, power, or oppression in their identities add or contribute to the conflict in the present? How did it help to escalate or de-escalate the conflict?

Return to the 10C's Model... How does this Model for Awareness and Change help us better understand and manage the conflict and tension that arises for us as leaders in schools and communities, as individuals partnering across differences to do the work of racial justice and health equity?

Example Four:
Circles of Power, Privilege, and Oppression – 10C' Circles

Goal: Give participants the opportunity to explore their 10C's by discussing the answers to the questions asked of them and their partners.

Procedure:

*Each person will be a part of one of two concentric circles. Draw a person in the **inner** circle that is facing **out**. Also, draw a person in the **outer** circle, which is facing the person in the **inner** circle. Both people will face one another at the same center point and **become a pair.***

Each partner will have 2-3 minutes to answer and discuss one question from the list below. At the end of the 2-3 minutes, they will then be asked to stop.

The people in the inner circle will then be asked to move one space to the right or left so they will have a different partner for each question.

They are to focus on the conversation between the two of them only. They should not pay attention to any other conversations in the room.

When the partners have finished, they should return to the larger group to process the following questions:

- *What was it like for you to discuss and answer the questions?*

- *Which questions were difficult to answer and why?*

- *Which questions were easy to answer and why?*

- *Were the questions easy or hard to answer and discuss, based on who you were talking to?*

- *What did people **do** that made you feel like you were heard?*

10 C's Concentric Circles Questions

Discuss three things about yourself you are proud of.

*Discuss three things about your racial or ethnic background of which you are proud. Talk about three things (other than food) about another racial or ethnic group **other than your own** that you admire or respect.*

Describe your earliest memory of racial, ethnic, color, or sexual difference.

***What** information did you get about those differences? Was it negative or positive? **How** did you get that information? Was it from adults, the media, books, or something else?*

*Describe an image or character you have seen on TV or in the movies that you think is **stereotypical** and explain why. How do you feel when you hear someone speaking a language other than your own? ("Concentric Circle Activity - ioby")*

Describe a time when someone you knew stopped doing something because of race, ethnicity, gender, age, or sexual orientation. How did you respond? Were you pleased with your response? If yes, why or if not, why?

What is your biggest concern about dealing with issues due to prejudice, stereotyping, and/or discrimination?

Describe a time when you felt confident and courageous about your C's. Which C's were they and why?

Talk about a time when you were in a conflict with someone. If it turned out to be a positive experience, explain why. If it was a negative experience, explain why. In both cases, talk about which

Example Five:
5 C's of Awareness Journal Topics

Color

Describe the color of your mother's or father's skin in the late summer.

Describe a physical feature that you think receives too much attention.

How does your birth order affect your personality?
Is intelligence innate?

How does your gender affect your leadership?

Write something that shows intelligence other than a linguistic example.

Describe your skin color and what you like and admire about it.

Describe the color of another person's skin other than your own that you like and what you admire about it.

Write about your early memories of color, gender, age, sexual orientation, class, or religious differences. Then explain why and how people were treated because of these differences.

Write about your racial identity. What do you like about it, and what do you dislike?

Write about the relationship between the colors white, black, brown, and yellow and how they are used to describe people.

<u>Culture</u>

Describe any object of your choosing, thoroughly using all five senses. Write about an object that means something to you without describing it

Describe yourself or a member of your family using only nouns and verbs.

Describe what you would be like if you grew up with a different parent.

Describe an object without using the sense of sight.

Describe an experience of God.

Describe your culture and what you like and admire about it. Describe a culture other than your own that you like and

admire.

Write about your early memories of cultural differences and

why and how people were treated because of these differences.

Write about what your culture says about your racial identity.

What do you like and do not like about this?

Write about the relationship between the colors white, black, brown, and yellow and how they are used to describe people from your culture's perspective.

<u>Class</u>

Describe a place that no one in the room knows you have.
been to—that says something about your societal access to
power.

What is the purpose of education?

What is one educational fad or trend that you think has worked
well?

Describe your relationship with authority.

Can anyone rise above or fall below their class? Who has

Who is the most powerful person in the world? Why?
Describe your class status and what you like and admire about
this status. Describe class status other than your own that you
like
and admire.

Write about your early memories of class differences, as
well as why and how people were treated because of
these differences.

Write about what your class says about your racial identity.
What do you like and do not like about
this?

Write about the relationship between the colors white, black,
brown, and yellow and how they are used to describe people's
reactions to class.

<u>Character</u>

What is one aspect of yourself that you have changed for the better?

Describe the process of authoring the best paper, letter, report or essay you have ever written.

Author a poem or paragraph that creates a character (think traits, e.g., habits, mannerisms, speech, goals).

Author a poem or paragraph about your greatest fear.

Write two poems to experiment with rhythm—one that is short and choppy (lots of stresses and one-syllable words) and then one that is long and flowing (musical and unstressed syllables)

Describe your character and what you like and admire about yourself.

Describe the character of someone other than yourself that you like and admire.

Write about your early memories of character differences, as well as why and how people were treated because of these differences.

Write about what your character says about your racial identity. What do you like and do not like about this.

Write about the relationship between the colors white, black, brown, and yellow and how they are used to describe people in relation to their character.

Context

Describe a person who influences you. Describe someone with whom you would LEAST like to spend an hour with.

Write about someone else in the room and what makes them tick.

What event changed your life? What about your parents' lives

Fill in the blank and explain: If ___________ did not happen, everything would be different.

Describe the context, time, and location in which you are presently located and what you like and admire about it.

Describe a time, or place that you like and admire.

Write about your early memories of where you grew up as a child. How were people treated because of their differences?

Write about your parents or other adults in your life when you

*were a child growing up. What did they say about your racial iden-
tity? What do you like and do not like about what they said?*

*Write about when you were a child and how you did or did not see
the relationship between the colors white, black, brown, and yellow. and how they are used to describe people in relation to their
character.*

<u>Other Questions</u>

Write about a place from the point of view of an object there (internal spectator).

Describe a famous place and your personal experience that is different from the normal one.

Describe an idea that challenges the normal societal point of view (e.g., "beauty is bad" or "money is useless"). Be sure to show, not tell.

Do you believe in Heaven or Hell? Why or why not?

Fill in the blank and explain: Would people do ________________ (use your imagination) if they could not tell anyone else about it?

What is the one thing in life that bothers you the most?

Describe the methods you use to relieve stress or work out your frustrations

What animal would you be if you could and why?

In what ways would you change your parents if you could? Describe someone who is quite different from the job they do.

Describe someone who is judged by the worst thing they ever did. Describe a painting or photograph you love to look at.

Describe a painting or photograph that disturbed you the first time you saw it.

Discuss a TV show or movie that gave you nightmares when you were younger.

What is your favorite class ever? Why?

Describe a person who used to be your friend. Will you ever be friends again?
What is your biggest fear and why?

Describe the last time you were in the middle of a fight or disagreement. What did you do?

What is the worst movie ever?

Write the dialogue of a fight or a difficult conversation you have had recently. Describe an instance of beauty in an unusual spot.

Writing about something ordinary that happened over spring break makes it extraordinary

Write about something ordinary that happened with the purpose of making it exciting.

Outline a plot for a story from event to event.

What is the best (or worst) short story you have ever read and why?

Why do authors draft short stories instead of novels?

What is the purpose of art?

What kind of parent will you be?

What is the most important thing in your life?

What is something few people know about you?

What is a talent you wish you had?

Write a letter (real or imagined) to an eighth grader about what you wish you had known the first year.

What were your first impressions of Hotchkiss? How did those change over the years?

Has Hotchkiss changed in the time you have been here? In what ways?

What is your biggest fear about college?

Why do people watch tv game shows or court shows?

____

____

____

____

____

____

____

Epilogue

Love is a complex and multifaceted human emotion that can be described as a strong affection or attachment towards someone or something. It is often characterized by feelings of warmth, tenderness, and care, and can be expressed in various ways through actions, words, and physical touch. Love can also come in different forms, such as romantic love, familial love, and platonic love. It is a fundamental aspect of human experience and has been the subject of art, literature, music, and philosophy for centuries.

The relationship between love of oneself and racial identity is complex and multifaceted and can vary depending on individual experiences and cultural contexts. On one hand, a powerful sense of self-love and self-acceptance can help individuals to develop a positive racial identity, which can foster a sense of belonging and pride in one's cultural heritage. By embracing their racial identity, individuals can gain a greater appreciation for the diversity and richness of their cultural traditions and history and can develop a greater sense of empathy and understanding towards others who may have different racial or cultural backgrounds.

On the other hand, racial identity can also be shaped by external factors such as discrimination, racism, and prejudice, which can lead to negative self-perceptions and a sense of inferiority or shame. In such cases, it can be difficult to cultivate a sense of self-love and acceptance, and individuals may struggle with feelings of anger, resentment, or internalized oppression.

It is important to note that self-love and racial identity are not mutually exclusive and that developing a positive sense of self-love can be an important aspect of cultivating a strong and positive racial identity. By embracing and celebrating their racial iden-

tity, individuals can gain a greater sense of self-worth and empowerment and can work towards building a more equitable and just society for all.

Moreover, self-love and racial identity are interrelated in the sense that a positive sense of self-love can help individuals overcome the negative effects of discrimination and prejudice and can lead to greater resilience and psychological well-being. When individuals have a positive self-concept, they are more likely to resist internalizing negative messages about their racial identity and are better able to cope with the stressors associated with racism and discrimination. This can help to promote a sense of personal agency and empowerment, which can in turn facilitate positive changes at the individual and societal levels.

Additionally, it is important to acknowledge that self-love and racial identity can intersect with other aspects of identity, such as gender, sexuality, and socioeconomic status. For example, individuals who belong to marginalized groups may face intersecting forms of oppression that can make it even more challenging to cultivate a positive sense of self-love and acceptance. In such cases, it is important to recognize the unique experiences and challenges faced by individuals from diverse backgrounds and to work towards creating inclusive and supportive environments that promote positive self-concepts and strong racial identities.

It is also important to recognize that self-love and racial identity are not fixed or static but rather can evolve and change over time. For example, individuals may experience shifts in their racial identity as they learn more about their cultural heritage or as they encounter new experiences and perspectives. Similarly, individuals may experience fluctuations in their sense of self-love and acceptance, depending on their life circumstances and emotional state.

Therefore, it is important to approach self-love and racial identity as ongoing processes of growth and development, rather than fixed states of being. This can involve engaging in practices such as self-reflection, self-care, and community building, which can help to promote greater self-awareness and self-acceptance. It can also involve seeking out resources and support networks, such as therapy, mentorship, or cultural organizations, which can help individuals to navigate the complexities of their racial identity and cultivate a positive sense of self-love and acceptance.

In conclusion, the relationship between self-love and racial identity is complex and multifaceted and can be influenced by a range of internal and external factors. By working towards developing a positive sense of self-love and embracing their racial identity, individuals can promote greater psychological well-being and work towards building a more equitable and just society for all.

Conclusion

My personal journey of moving from seeing myself as defined by the dominant society to redefining my identities on my own terms has helped to reshape how I see myself and how I live my life.

The process of moving from awareness to self-transformation recognizes and celebrates the complexity of personal and professional relationships while providing an accessible language for discussing difficult issues of identity.

It shifts the conversation from a win/loses deficit approach to a win/win and asset-based one. It sees differences and similarities in the 10C's of everyone – C's that they both consciously and unconsciously bring to the relationship as a resource, not a problem.

It is a process that demands we "live the 10C's Model" as we experience the challenges and rewards of alliance building. The Model and the process are grounded in the belief that all people can change and in lofty expectations that people will act on their increasing knowledge and awareness.

My work as a counselor, educator, and advocate has blessed me with many opportunities to see and experience the power of dialogue to promote change. I bear witness to many people I have worked with using the 10C's focus process as they experience a sense of what is possible with their new awareness and appreciation for their 10C's.

They realize that if they can create an authentic experience in a counseling session, they can replicate it elsewhere in their lives. The Model is only an intellectual tool, but it comes alive when we act on the new awareness and knowledge we have gained and use the tools and skills we have learned in creative ways.

Bibliography

This is merely a suggested list of a few books with which to start your exploration of the problem of racism - White Supremacy.

Akbar, N. Chains and Images of Psychological Slavery. New Jersey: New Mind Productions, 1990.

Alexander, Michelle. The New Jim Crow. New York, NY: The New Press, 2010.

Aliport, Gordon. The Nature of Prejudice. Cambridge, Massachusetts: Addison Wesley, 1979.

Allen, J, Als H., J. Lewis, & L.F. Litwack Without Sanctuary: Lynching Photography in America. New Mexico: Twin Palms Publishers, 2000.

Burton, M. Garlinda. Never Say Nigger Again. Nashville TN 37205: James C. Winston, 1976.

Carter, Forrest. The Education of Little Tree. Albuquerque, New Mexico, 1986.

Chu, Louis. Eat a Bowl of Tea. New Jersey: Lyle Stuart, Inc., 1961.

Clark, Kenneth. Prejudice and Your Child. Middleton, Connecticut: Wesleyan, 1986.

Clavell, James. The Childen's Story. New York, 1981

Cobbe, Price, and Crier, William. Black Rage. New York: Basic Books, 1960.

Cone, James H. Martin, and Malcolm and American. Maryknoll, New York: Orbis Books, 1991.

Cose, Ellis. The Rage of a Privileged Class. New York, New York: Harper Collins, 1993.

DeGruy, Joy. _Post Traumatic Slave Syndrome_, Joy DeGruy Publishing, Portland OR, 2005.

Deloria, Vine. _Custer Died for Your Sins_. New York: Avon, 1970

Deloria, Vine. _God is Red_. New York: Dell, 1983

Deloria, Vine. _We Talk, You Listen_. New York: MacMillan, 1970.

Friedman, Thomas. _From Beirut to Jerusalem_. New York: Doubleday, 1989

Friedman, Thomas. _The World is Flat_. New York, NY: Farrar, Straus, and Giroux, 2005.

Gladwell, Malcolm. _Blink_. New York, NY: Little, Brown, and Co., 2005.

Glassner, Barry. _The Culture of Fear_. New York, NY: Basic Book, 1999.

Golden, Harry. _Enjoy! Enjoy!_ Cleveland: World, 1960

Golden, Harry. _For 2 Cent Plain_. Cleveland: World, 1959.

Golden, Harry. _Only in America_. Cleveland: World, 1959.

Grier, W. H. & P. H. Cobbs _Black Rage_. New York: Bantam

Books, 1969

Hecker, Andrew. _Two Nations: Black and White. Separate, Hostile, and Unequal_. MacMillan (H.B.) Ballantine (P.B.), 1992.

Homokawa, Bill. _The Quiet Americans_. New York: Morrow, 1972.

Houston, Jeane and James D. _Farewell to Manzanar_. New York, 1974.

Kane, Pearl Rock and Orsini, Alfonso, J. _The Color of Excellence._ New York, NY: Teachers College Press, Columbia Univ., 2003.

Kennedy, Randall. _Nigger_. New York, NY: Pantheon Books, 2002.

King, Martin Luther. _Strength to Love_, Fortress Press, Philadelphia, 1981

Kochman, Thomas. _Black and White Styles in Conflict_. Chicago: University of Chicago Press, 1981.

Kivel, Paul. _Uprooting Racism_, Canada, new Society Publishers, 2003.

Lakoff, George. _Don't Think of an Elephant. White River_ Junction, VT: Chelsea Green Pub Co., 2004

Landsman, Julie. _A White Teacher Talks About Race_. Lanham, Maryland: Scarecrow Press, Inc., 2001.

Lincoln, C. Eric. _Race, Religions and the Continuing American Dilemma_. New York, NY: Hill and Wang, 1999.

Loewen, James, W. _Lies My Teacher Told Me_. New York, NY: The New Press, 1995.

Mathabane, Mark. _Kaffir Boy_. New York: Macmillan, 1986.

Mirande, Alfredo. _The Chicago Experiment: An Alternative Perspective_. Notre Dame, 1985.

Morrison, Toni. _The Bluest Eye_. New York: Washington Square, 1972.

Nam, Vicki. _Yell-Oh Girls_. New York, NY: Harper Collins, 2001.

Pauling, Chris. _Introducing Buddhism_. New York, NY: Barnes and Noble Books, 1990.

Peters, William. _A Class Divided: Then and Now_. New Haven, Connecticut: Yale, 1987.

Pinderhoughes, E. _Understanding Race, Ethnicity, and Power_. New York: The Free Press, 1989.

Rodriguez, Richard. *Hunger of Memory: The Education of Richard Rodriguez*. New York: Bantam, 1982.

Ruiz, Don Miguel. *The Four Agreements*. San Rafael, CA: Amber-Allen Publishing, 1997.

Rutstein, Nathan. *The Racial Conditioning of our Children*. Albion, MI: The National Resource Center for the Healing of Racism, 2001.

Ryan, William. *Blaming the Victim*. New York: Random House, 1972.

Shipler, David K. *Arab and Jew*. New York: Penguin Books, 1986.

Siberman, Charles. *Crisis is Black and White*. New York: Random House, 1972.

Simons, Abramms, Hopkins, and Johnson. *Cultural Diversity*. Princeton, NJ: Peterson's/Pacesetter Books, 1996

Smith, Lillian. *Killers of the Dream*. New York: Norton, 1978.

Stern-LaRosa, and Bettman, Ellen H. *Hate Hurts*. New York, NY: Scholastic, Inc., 2000.

Stevenson. H.C. *Relationship of Adolescent Perception of Racial Identity*. Journal of Black Psychology, 21 (1) 49-70 1994.

Stiglitz, Joseph E. *The Price of Inequality*. New York: Norton, 2012.

Tan, Amy. *The Kitchen God's Wife*. G.P. Putnam's Sons, 1991.

Tatum, B. D. *Why Are all the Black Kids Sitting Together in the Cafeteria?* New York: Basic Books, 1997.

Urrea, Luis Alberto. *Across the Wire: Life and Hard Times on the Mexican Border*. New York: Anchor Books, 1993.

Urrea, Luis Alberto. *The Devil's Highway*. New York, NY: Little,

Brown, and Co., 2004.

Walker, Alice. _The Color Purple_. New York: Washington Square, 1982.

Walsh, Joan. _What's the Matter with White People_. New Jersey: John Wiley & Sons, 2012.

Wattenberg, Ben. _Birth Dearth_. New York: Pharos, 1987.

Weatherford, Jack. Native Roots. New York, NY: Ballantine Books, 1991.

West, C. _Race Matters._ Boston, MA. Beacon Press, 1993.

White, Joseph L. _The Psychology of Blacks_. Englewood Cliffs, New Jersey: Prentice Hall, Inc., 1984.

Williams A. _KWANZAA THE SEVEN PRINCIPLES_, Peter Pauper Press Inc. White Plain, New York, 1996.

William, Eric. _History of the People of Trinidad and Tobago_, A&B Books Publishers Brooklyn, New York, 1942.

Williams, Juan. _Eyes on the Prize_. New York: Viking, 1987.

Wright, Richard. _Black Boy_. New York: Harper and Row, 1969.

Yette, Samuel F. _Choice: The Issue of Black Survival in America_. Springs, Maryland: Cottage Books, 1982.

Zinn, Howard. _A People's History of the United States_. New York: Harper Collins Publishers, 1990.

About the Author

Dr. Ulric Johnson *is a community organizer focusing on the impact of "isms" and violence on youth, families, organizations, and communities. He specializes in the impact of color, culture, class, character, and context on individual and group behaviors, especially as it relates to the prevention, progression, and treatment of what he refers to as addictive behaviors.*

He runs a private group practice Transformation Awareness Growth Vision. Where he and his associates provide anti racism, cross cultural mental health counseling, coaching and consultation, as well as the founder and director of Teens Against Gang Violence, a peer leadership, youth, and family program.

Dr. Johnson is the former Assistant Dean/Campus Director of Springfield College: Boston Campus School of Human Services, Co-founder of the Peaceable Schools and Community Group, a former faculty member of the Harvard Graduate School of Education and the Lesley College Center for Peaceable Schools and Communities.

Dr. Johnson received his PhD in Cross-Cultural Psychology from Southwestern University and his M.A. in Psychology from Boston College.

He is a Board-Certified Human Service Professional, Certified Addiction Specialist, Certified AIDS Counselor, Certified Forensic Counselor, Licensed Alcohol and Drug Counselor, Licensed Mental Health Counselor, Licensed Rehabilitation Counselor, and Licensed Marriage and Family Therapist.

Dr. Johnson is a local, national, and international organizer, presenter, consultant, and trainer on Cross-Cultural and Multicultural Communication and Relationship, Gang Violence Prevention, and Youth Leadership Development. He is actively involved in his local community in developing coalitions and collaborative work in bringing a multicultural approach to the issues of urban violence from a Public Health perspective.

He can be contacted at:

Phone: *(617)365-0637,* ***Email:*** *Ulric J@aol.com*